Collins
Common
Errors
in English

AND HOW TO AVOID THEM

HarperCollins Publishers
Westerhill Road
Bishopbriggs
Glasgow
G64 2QT

First Edition 2013

Reprint 10 9 8 7 6 5 4 3 2 1 0

© HarperCollins Publishers 2013

ISBN 978-0-00-750612-5

Collins® is a registered trademark
of HarperCollins Publishers Limited

www.collinslanguage.com

A catalogue record for this book is
available from the British Library

Typeset by
Davidson Publishing Solutions

Printed in Great Britain by Clays Ltd,
St Ives plc

Acknowledgements
We would like to thank those
authors and publishers who kindly
gave permission for copyright
material to be used in the Collins
Corpus. We would also like to thank
Times Newspapers Ltd for providing
valuable data.

WRITTEN BY
Elizabeth Walter
Kate Woodford

EDITOR
Gerry Breslin

FOR THE PUBLISHER
Lucy Cooper
Kerry Ferguson
Elaine Higgleton

Contents

Introduction

Collins Common Errors in English is a practical guide to the mistakes that learners of English often make and how to avoid them. Whether you are preparing for an exam, writing an essay, or you simply want to make sure that your English is as accurate as possible, *Collins Common Errors in English* offers you the information you need in a clear and accessible form.

This book is in several parts:

- The first sections are organized by part of speech. In short, clear paragraphs, they explain the most common errors connected with each part of speech. For instance, the section on *verbs* covers areas such as using the correct preposition after a verb, and how to avoid mistakes with modal verbs and phrasal verbs. These sections also include information on tenses and making sentences.

- The next sections focus on choosing the right word. There are many reasons why it can be easy to confuse words. It may be because they sound the same or look similar (eg board/bored, desert/dessert), because they have similar but slightly different meanings (eg continual/ continuous, blame/fault), or because it is easy to confuse the different parts of speech (eg breath and breathe). Many mistakes are made because of a confusion with another language (eg actual/current, library/bookshop), and these sections deal with those errors too.

- After this come the topic sections, which cover areas which are often prone to a lot of mistakes, such as time, travel, and numbers. For each of these, clear information is given to help you talk about the topics confidently and accurately.

- Finally, you will find information on common mistakes with punctuation and spelling, followed by several pages of exercises which you can use to test what you have learned or to see where you need more help.

Within each section, mistakes are introduced with clear headings. There is also a comprehensive index and a helpful glossary at the end of the book to help you find all the information you need.

For more information about Collins dictionaries, you can visit us at **www.collinslanguage.com**.

Verbs

Verb patterns

Verb + *to*- infinitive

> *We agreed to go to his house.*
> ~~We agreed go to his house.~~

> *I managed to finish the painting.*
> ~~I managed finishing the painting.~~

Here is a list of common verbs that are used with a *to*- infinitive, and rarely or never with an infinitive without *to* or an *-ing* verb:

afford	decide	hope	promise
agree	demand	intend	refuse
aim	deserve	learn	seem
appear	expect	manage	tend
arrange	fail	mean	threaten
ask	fight	need	wait
attempt	forget	offer	want
choose	grow	plan	wish
claim	help	prepare	
dare	hesitate	pretend	

Verb + object + *to*- infinitive

> *They invited her to speak at the conference.*
> ~~They invited her for speaking at the conference.~~

> *I asked him to close the door.*
> ~~I asked him close the door.~~

Here is a list of common verbs that are used with an object and a *to*- infinitive, and rarely or never with an infinitive without *to* or a preposition + *-ing* verb:

advise	encourage	order	train
allow	expect	pay	trust
ask	forbid	persuade	want
beg	force	prefer	warn
cause	get	remind	
choose	help	teach	
enable	invite	tell	

Verb + object + infinitive without *to*

I made him listen.
~~I made him to listen.~~

He let me come with him.
~~He let me coming with him.~~

Make (meaning 'force') and *let* are followed by an object and an infinitive without *to*. Do not use *to* and do not use an *-ing* verb.

Verb + *-ing* verb

They are considering moving to France.
~~They are considering move to France.~~

She kept asking me to help her.
~~She kept to ask me to help her.~~

Here is a list of common verbs that are used with an *-ing* verb, and rarely or never with an infinitive:

admit	describe	imagine	mind
appreciate	dislike	keep	miss
avoid	enjoy	like	risk
consider	fancy	look forward to	stand
delay	finish	love	stop
deny	hate	mention	suggest

Note also the following phrases:

I **can't stand** getting up early.
I **don't feel** like going out tonight.

I **can't help** feeling sorry for him.
I **don't mind** waiting.

Verb + object + *-ing* verb

I stopped him getting in the car.
~~I stopped him to get in the car.~~

I caught her looking at my email.
~~I caught her look at my email.~~

Here is a list of common verbs that are used with an object and an *-ing* verb, and rarely or never with an infinitive:

catch	imagine	prevent	stop
find	notice	see	watch
hear	picture	spot	

Remember to do *or* remember doing?

Remember to lock the door.
~~Remember locking the door.~~

Do you remember meeting Joe?
~~Do you remember to meet Joe?~~

A few verbs have different patterns for different meanings. If you *remember to do* something, you do not forget to do it, and if you *remember doing* something you still have a memory of it.

The verb *forget* is similar. If you *forget to do* something, you do not remember to do it, and if you *have forgotten doing* something, you no longer have a memory of it.

Similarly, you use *try + to-* infinitive to say that you make an effort to do something, and *try + -ing* verb to talk about doing something to see how useful, effective, or enjoyable it is:

I tried **to cheer** him up.
Have you **tried talking** to him about the problem?

Verbs + it

I hate it when you laugh at me.

~~I hate when you laugh at me.~~

I would appreciate it if you could
reply soon.
~~I would appreciate if you could
reply soon.~~

Verbs such as *like*, *hate*, *dislike*, and *love* (which are used to say how you feel about an event or a situation), need the word *it* when they are followed by *when* or *if*.

However, you do not use *it* when you follow one of these verbs with an infinitive verb or an *-ing* verb:

I like walking in the park.
~~I like it walking in the park.~~

I like to see my friends.
~~I like it to see my friends.~~

You should also use *it* with *find* in sentences about your experiences:

I **found it** difficult to get to know him.
She **found it** amusing to watch us struggle.

I suggest/recommend that you …

I suggest that you go to London.
~~I suggest you to go to London.~~

I recommend that you take the train.
~~I recommend you to take the train.~~

Do not say that you *suggest/recommend* someone to do something. Say that you *suggest/recommend that* they do something.

I'm thinking of + *-ing* verb

I'm thinking of leaving home.
~~I'm thinking to leave home.~~

They were thinking of inviting Moya.
~~They were thinking to invite Moya.~~

If you are considering doing something, you can say that you are *thinking of doing* it. Do not say that you are *thinking to do* something.

Wish + past tense

I wish I had more friends.
~~I wish I have more friends.~~

I wish I had sold my car.
~~I wish I have sold my car.~~

Use a past tense in the part of the sentence that comes after *I wish*, not a present tense.

Can see/hear/feel, etc.

I can hear an owl.
~~I hear an owl.~~

I can taste the garlic.
~~I taste the garlic.~~

You usually use *can* before verbs connected with the senses.

Afford

We can afford to take a taxi.
~~We afford to take a taxi.~~

We were able to afford a new television.
~~We afforded a new television.~~

Afford is almost always used after *can*, *could*, or *be able to*.

Prepositions after verbs

Choosing the right preposition

It depends on the weather.
~~It depends of the weather.~~

We arrived at the hotel in the evening.
~~We arrived to the hotel in the evening.~~

Some verbs are followed by a particular preposition and it is important to use the right one.

Here are some more verb + preposition combinations that are often used incorrectly:

*They **accused** her **of** lying. (Not ~~accuse for~~)*
*She doesn't **approve of** my friends. (Not ~~approve to~~)*
*He **complained about** the noise. (Not ~~complain over~~)*
*I **rely on** the money I get from selling vegetables. (Not ~~rely of~~)*
*We need to **talk about** your education. (Not ~~talk of~~)*

When is a preposition needed?

She explained to me that the hotel was closed.
~~She explained me that the hotel was closed.~~

That book belongs to Harry.

~~That book belongs Harry.~~

Some verbs always need a preposition before an object, and you should not use them without it.

Here are some more examples of verbs that must have a preposition when they are used with an object:

*He **agreed with** me.*
*They **apologized for** their mistake.*
*We **disposed of** the waste materials.*
*The thief **escaped from** prison.*
*I love **listening to** music.*
*I'm **looking for** a pen.*
*She was **searching for** her keys.*
*He **suggested to** me that we should go by train.*
*I'm **waiting for** an important call.*

Note also the following verbs, which always need a preposition after the object where there is also an indirect object:

*He **described** the room **to** me.*
*I **invited** her **to** my party.*
*They **provided** me **with** the equipment I needed.*

When is a preposition not needed?

He told me that he was a doctor.   *We left the party at eleven o'clock.*
~~*He told to me that he was a doctor.*~~   ~~*We left from the party at eleven o'clock.*~~

Some verbs do not need a preposition before an object, and you should not put one in.

Look at these examples:

*She **answered me** politely. (Not ~~answer to~~)*
*Max **approached the man**. (Not ~~approach to~~)*
*I **asked Maria** what time it was. (Not ~~ask to~~)*
*I **called him** last night. (Not ~~call to~~)*
*The book **lacked an index**. (Not ~~lack of~~)*
*He **married a woman** from Cambridge. (Not ~~marry to~~)*
*I need some trousers to **match this jacket.** (Not ~~match to~~)*
*We didn't **reach the hotel** until midnight. (Not ~~reach to~~)*
*They **requested a copy** of the document. (Not ~~request for~~)*
*I **returned the book** I had borrowed. (Not ~~return back~~)*

Verb + preposition + -ing

He kept on working.   *We thought of inviting Max.*
~~*He kept on to work.*~~   ~~*We thought of to invite Max.*~~

When a verb is followed by a preposition, the verb that follows it is usually in the -ing form.

Look at these examples:

*He **dreamed of becoming** an actor.*
*She **carried on talking**.*
*She **insisted on walking** all the way.*

Where to put the preposition

I gave the money to Marc.   *I bought a toy for the child.*
~~*I gave to Marc the money.*~~   ~~*I bought for the child a toy.*~~

When you use a verb with two objects, you should put the preposition and the indirect object after the direct object.

Modal verbs (can, must, should, etc.)

Modal verb + main verb without to

I'm glad you can come to my wedding.
I'm glad you can to come to my wedding.

I must buy some more milk.
I must to buy some more milk.

The modal verbs *can*, *could*, *may*, *might*, *must*, *should*, *shall*, *will*, and *would* are followed by the base form of a verb without *to*.

However, we do use *to* after *ought*:

*You **ought to** go to the doctor.*

Ought to/should/must + present perfect

It ought to have finished by now.

It ought to finish by now.

I'm a bit worried about Rebecca.
She should have arrived by now.

I'm a bit worried about Rebecca.
She should arrive by now.

If you use the modal verbs *ought to*, *should*, or *must* to talk about something that was expected to happen by now, use the present perfect and not the infinitive after the modal verb.

Must or have to?

Will you have to do all the work?
Will you must do all the work?

I didn't have to pay.
I didn't must pay.

Must is never used in negative sentences or in questions formed with *will*, *do*, or *have*.

Mustn't or don't have to?

I don't have to go to work today.
I mustn't go to work today.

Luckily, we don't have to pay.
Luckily, we mustn't pay.

Mustn't or *must not* is used to say that it is important that something is not done. If you want to say that it is not necessary that something is done, you use *don't have to*.

Mustn't be *or* can't be?

He can't be her dad because he's too
    young.
He mustn't be her dad because he's too
    young.

The two statements can't both be
    correct.
The two statements mustn't both
    be correct.

To say that you believe something is not true, use *cannot* or *can't*. Do not
use *must not* or *mustn't*.

Would you like …?

Would you like to come out tonight?
Would you like come out tonight?

Would you like to eat now?
Do you like to eat now?

When you start an offer or a suggestion with *Would you like …?*, it has to be
followed by a *to-* infinitive.

Do not use *do you like* for making an offer or suggestion. Use *do you like* to
ask about someone's opinion of something:

Do you like Chinese food?

Used to

We didn't use to have a TV.
We didn't used to have a TV.

I'm not used to speaking in public.
I didn't used to speaking in public.

If something *used to* happen, it happened regularly in the past, but does not
happen now. When you make negative sentences or questions, you write
use to instead of *used to*:

I didn't **use to** see much of him.
Did you **use to** play football?

Note that *used to* has another meaning. If you are *used to* something, you
have become familiar with it and you accept it. With this sense, *used to* has
the verb *be* or *get* in front of it, and is followed by a noun or an *-ing* form:

He's **used to** hard work.
I'm **used to** get**ting** up early.

Using special types of verb

Using reflexive verbs

He enjoyed himself at the concert.
He enjoyed him at the concert.

She taught herself to speak French.
She taught her to speak French.

You use a reflexive pronoun to talk about a situation where the same person is involved as both the subject and the object of an action. Make sure you use the correct form of the pronoun: *myself*, *yourself*, *himself*, *herself*, *itself*, *ourselves*, and *themselves*.

When reflexives are not needed

He got up and got dressed.
He got up and dressed himself.

Would you like to have a wash?
Would you like to wash yourself?

Note that reflexive pronouns are not used as much in English as in some other languages when talking about actions that you do to yourself.

Instead, use phrases such as *have a shave/bath*, etc. or *get dressed*.

Linking verb + adjective

It tastes good.
It tastes well.

She looked sad.
She looked sadly.

Do not use adverbs after linking verbs such as *be*, *seem*, *look*, *smell*, and *taste*.

Verbs without passive forms

The book consists of ten chapters.
The book was consisted of ten chapters.

We weren't allowed to take photos.
We weren't let take photos.

The verbs *let* and *consist of* are never used in the passive. The verb *get* is not usually used in the passive in formal English. Other verbs that are never, or very rarely, used in the passive are *have*, *like*, *resemble*, and *suit*.

Phrasal verbs

Position of pronouns with phrasal verbs

> You need to clean it up.
> ~~You need to clean up it.~~

> The noise woke me up.
> ~~The noise woke up me.~~

The object of a transitive phrasal verb can usually be put in front of the particle or after it:

> Don't give **the story** away.
> Don't give away **the story**.

However, when the object of the verb is a pronoun such as *me*, *him*, or *them*, the pronoun must always go in front of the particle.

Using phrasal verbs instead of formal verbs

> You shouldn't have to put up with such rudeness.
> ~~You shouldn't have to tolerate such rudeness.~~

> I went with him to the party.
> ~~I accompanied him to the party.~~

Although some phrasal verbs are informal, many are neutral, and are used much more commonly that the corresponding single-word verb. Using a single-word verb instead can make your English sound very formal and unnatural.

Here are some examples of formal verbs, where the phrasal verb is used more often:

accelerate → speed up
accumulate → build up
calculate → work out
cohabit → live together
conceal → cover up
decelerate → slow down
descend → come down
discard → throw away
dismantle → take apart
emerge → come out
emit → give off
encounter → come across
enter → come in

erase → rub out
establish → set up
exhale → breathe out
exit → go out
experience → go through
extinguish → put out
fasten → do up
illuminate → light up
incorporate → build in
indicate → point out
inflate → blow up
inhale → breathe in
intervene → step in

introduce → bring in
investigate → look into
omit → leave out
participate → join in
postpone → put off
proceed → go ahead
protrude → stick out
relinquish → give up
renovate → do up
reprimand → tell off

request → ask for
retaliate → fight back
revolve → go round
ridicule → laugh at
subside → die down
subtract → take away
surrender → give in
tolerate → put up with
transmit → pass on
withhold → keep back

Tenses

Present tenses

Present progressive, not present simple

> I can't come now – I'm having dinner.
> ~~I can't come now – I have my dinner.~~

> I'm studying at the moment.
> ~~I study at the moment.~~

The present progressive (*am/is/are* + *-ing* participle) is used to talk about a temporary situation in the present. Do not use the present simple to describe a temporary situation.

Compare these examples:

> I **listen** to all sorts of music in my spare time.
> I'**m listening** to a lot of jazz at the moment.

> Ben **works** in London.
> Ben'**s working** in London for six months.

> We often **have** a cup of coffee together.
> Come and join us! – We'**re having** a cup of coffee.

Present simple, not present progressive

> He catches the train every day.
> ~~He is catching the train every day.~~

> It snows a lot in January.
> ~~It is snowing a lot in January.~~

The present simple is used to talk about things that often or sometimes happen, and things that are always or generally true. Do not use the present progressive for either of these.

Look at these examples:

> I **see** Alice most days.
> John **works** abroad.
> I'**m** very fond of Phoebe.
> She **doesn't** smoke.
> The west of the country **gets** more rainfall.

Adverbs of frequency with the present simple

> I always take my umbrella.
> ~~Always I take my umbrella.~~

> I'm never late for appointments.
> ~~Never I'm late for appointments.~~

In the present simple, adverbs such as *always*, *often*, *usually*, and *never* usually go before the verb in a sentence. If the verb is *to be*, however, they go after it. The adverbs *often* and *usually* can also go at the beginning or, less commonly, at the end of the sentence. The adverbs *always* and *never* do not appear at the start of a sentence.

Verbs not used in the progressive form

> *I don't believe her.*
> ~~*I am not believing her.*~~

> *She seems happy.*
> ~~*She is seeming happy.*~~

Some verbs are never, or very rarely, used in the progressive form. Many of them belong to certain categories, for example, verbs that relate to the senses and verbs that express belief and preference. Here is a list of common verbs that are not usually used in the progressive form:

agree	dislike	like	recognize
be	doubt	love	remember
believe	fit	mean	seem
belong	hate	need	sell
come from	hear	owe	sound
contain	imagine	own	suppose
cost	include	prefer	surprise
depend	involve	promise	understand
disagree	know	realize	want

Note that some verbs are not used in the progressive form with one meaning but are used in the progressive form with other meanings. Here are some of the most important ones, with the meaning that is never used in the progressive:

> *It feels strange to be back in my old classroom.*
> ~~*It is feeling strange to be back in my old classroom.*~~

> *I think she's wrong about that.*
> ~~*I am thinking she's wrong about that.*~~

> *She looks sad to me.*
> ~~*She is looking sad to me.*~~

> *I see what you mean.*
> ~~*I am seeing what you mean.*~~

> *This tastes absolutely delicious.*
> ~~*This is tasting absolutely delicious.*~~

Past tenses

Past simple: questions and negatives

I didn't see Greg.
I didn't saw Greg.

Did you speak to Isabel?
Did you spoke to Isabel?

To make a negative statement in the past simple, you put *did not* or *didn't* after the subject, and then you use the bare infinitive of the verb. Do not use the past tense of the verb:

We **didn't go** there in the end.
She **didn't tell** us where to meet.

To make a question in the past simple, you put *did* before the subject, and then you use the bare infinitive of the verb. Do not use the past tense of the verb:

Did you **have** nice food there?
Did Alex **give** you the book?

Note that *did* and *didn't* are the same with all pronouns.

Since *or* for

I've lived here for ten years.

I've lived here since ten years.

I've been waiting here for two
    hours!
I've been waiting here since two
    hours!

To say how long something has continued to the present time, you use *for* plus a period of time, or *since* plus a date or time in the past. Do not confuse *for* with *since*.

Look at these examples:

I've been working **since** six o'clock this morning.
I've lived here **since** 2008.
I've been learning the piano **for** three years now.
We've known each other **for** over ten years.

To say how long something has continued to the present time, you must use a perfect form:

> I**'ve lived** here since 2008.
> I**'ve been seeing** Sean for six months.

Note that you can use *from* and *to* in the same sentence, but not *since* and *to*:

> He worked here **from** 2005 **to** 2009.

Note also that you do not use *during* plus a period of time to say how long something has continued to the present. You use *for* for this.

Already/still/yet

> I'm still waiting for my luggage.
> ~~I'm yet waiting for my luggage.~~
>
> Karen has already finished.
> ~~Karen has finished yet.~~

Still is used to say that a situation continues to exist:

> I'm **still** hoping Peter will be able to come.
> Do you **still** play the guitar?

Do not confuse *still* with *yet* which is used in negative sentences to say that something has not happened up to the present time:

> I haven't called her **yet**.
> It isn't even dark **yet**.

Do not confuse *yet* with *already* which is used to say that something has happened before now, or that it has happened sooner than expected:

> I've eaten **already**, thank you.
> We've only walked a kilometer and I'm **already** exhausted!

Present perfect *or* past simple?

> She flew to Paris yesterday.
>
> ~~She's flown to Paris yesterday.~~
>
> I went to Susie's party a couple of months ago.
> ~~I've been to Susie's party a couple of months ago.~~

When you talk about an event that started and finished in the past and you say exactly when it happened, you must use the past simple and not the present perfect. Compare these examples:

*I'm hungry – I **didn't have** breakfast this morning.*
*I'm hungry – I **haven't eaten** all day.*

*I **didn't see** Oliver at the weekend.*
*I **haven't seen** Oliver for ages.*

Note, however, that with the present perfect you can use an adverb that shows how long a situation or event lasts or takes, such as *always* or *forever*:

*I've finished school **forever**.*
*I've **always** loved music.*

Similarly, if you ask when an event in the past happened, you must use the past simple.

*When **did** you **get** your car?*
*What time **did** you **get** here?*

Present perfect/present perfect progressive *or* present simple/present progressive?

Julia is a good friend – I've known her for years.
~~Julia is a good friend – I know her for years.~~

I've been learning the guitar for three years.
~~I'm learning the guitar for three years.~~

If you talk about how long an event or a situation has continued when that event started in the past and has continued until the present, you must use the present perfect or the present perfect progressive. Do not use the present simple or the present progressive for this:

*I**'ve lived** in the same apartment now for over six years.*
*I'm fed up. I**'ve been waiting** here for over an hour.*

Similarly, if you ask how long an event or a situation has continued when that event started in the past and has continued until the present, you must use the present perfect or the present perfect progressive:

*How long **have** you **been married**?*
*How long **have** you **been seeing** Ian?*

Past perfect *or* past simple?

By the time we got there, they had left.

~~By the time we got there, they left.~~

We weren't hungry because we'd already eaten.

~~We weren't hungry because we already ate.~~

If you want to talk about a past event or situation that occurred before a particular time in the past, you use the past perfect (*had* + past participle) and not the past simple.

Future tenses

Will, going to, *or* present progressive?

We're going to see the new Bond movie tonight.

~~We will see the new Bond movie tonight.~~

Isabel is flying to the US next week.

~~Isabel will fly to the US next week.~~

Going to is used far more than *will* to talk about intentions and plans:

I'm **going to** call Jo this evening and invite her.
We're **going to** fly to Edinburgh as it's so much quicker.
She's **going to** ask the teacher for help.

The present progressive (*am/is/are* + *-ing* participle) is used far more often than *will* to talk about plans:

I'm **leaving** in an hour.
We're **visiting** my parents this weekend.
I'm **having** my hair cut this afternoon.

Will is used to make predictions about the future:

Rachel **will** be so pleased with her present.
Jamie **won't** be happy when he hears the news.
I'm fairly confident Joe **will** pass his exams.

People also use *will* to announce plans at the point when they make those plans. Often, phrases such as *I think* and *perhaps* go before *will* when it is used in this way:

If you're going to the park, I'**ll** come too.
I think we'**ll** probably leave now, if that's all right.
Perhaps I'**ll** join you later.

Irregular verbs

Using the correct form of verbs

> I paid for the food.
> ~~I payed for the food.~~

> He has broken his leg.
> ~~He has broke his leg.~~

The usual way of forming past tenses is with -ed: *We played football. I have decided to go to London.* However, many common verbs have irregular past forms. Here are some of the most useful ones:

Verb	Past form	Passive/past perfect
be	was/were	been
beat	beat	beaten
become	became	become
begin	began	begun
bend	bent	bent
bet	bet	bet
bite	bit	bitten
bleed	bled	bled
blow	blew	blown
break	broke	broken
bring	brought	brought
build	built	built
burn	burned *or* burnt	burned *or* burnt
burst	burst	burst
buy	bought	bought
catch	caught	caught
choose	chose	chosen
come	came	come
cost	cost	cost
cut	cut	cut
deal	dealt	dealt
dig	dug	dug
draw	drew	drawn
dream	dreamed *or* dreamt	dreamed *or* dreamt
drink	drank	drunk
drive	drove	driven
eat	ate	eaten
fall	fell	fallen

Verb	Past form	Passive/past perfect
feed	fed	fed
feel	felt	felt
fight	fought	fought
find	found	found
fly	flew	flown
forbid	forbade	forbidden
forget	forgot	forgotten
forgive	forgave	forgiven
freeze	froze	frozen
get	got	got
give	gave	given
grow	grew	grown
hang	hung	hung
have	had	had
hear	heard	heard
hide	hid	hidden
hit	hit	hit
hold	held	held
hurt	hurt	hurt
keep	kept	kept
kneel	kneeled or knelt	kneeled or knelt
know	knew	known
lay	laid	laid
lead	led	led
lean	leaned or leant	leaned or leant
leap	leapt or leaped	leapt or leaped
learn	learned or learnt	learned or learnt
leave	left	left
lend	lent	lent
let	let	let
lie (on back)	lay	lain
light	lit or lighted	lit or lighted
lose	lost	lost
make	made	made
mean	meant	meant
meet	met	met
overcome	overcame	overcome
overtake	overtook	overtaken

Verb	Past form	Passive/past perfect
pay	paid	paid
prove	proved	proved or proven
put	put	put
quit	quit	quit
read	read	read
ride	rode	ridden
ring	rang	rung
rise	rose	risen
run	ran	run
say	said	said
see	saw	seen
sell	sold	sold
send	sent	sent
set	set	set
sew	sewed	sewn
shake	shook	shaken
shine	shone	shone
shoot	shot	shot
show	showed	shown or showed
shrink	shrank	shrunk
shut	shut	shut
sing	sang	sung
sink	sank	sunk
sit	sat	sat
sleep	slept	slept
slide	slid	slid
smell	smelled or smelt	smelled or smelt
speak	spoke	spoken
spell	spelled or spelt	spelled or spelt
spend	spent	spent
spill	spilled or spilt	spilled or spilt
spin	span	spun
spit	spat	spat
split	split	split
spoil	spoiled or spoilt	spoiled or spoilt
spread	spread	spread
stand	stood	stood
steal	stole	stolen

Verb	Past form	Passive/past perfect
stick	stuck	stuck
sting	stung	stung
swear	swore	sworn
sweep	swept	swept
swim	swam	swum
swing	swung	swung
take	took	taken
teach	taught	taught
tear	tore	torn
tell	told	told
think	thought	thought
throw	threw	thrown
tread	trod	trodden
understand	understood	understood
undo	undid	undone
upset	upset	upset
wake	woke	woken
wear	wore	worn
weep	wept	wept
win	won	won
wind	wound	wound
write	wrote	written

Nouns

Uncountable, mass, and plural nouns

Common uncountable nouns

This furniture is very old.
~~These furnitures are very old.~~

She gave me some good advice.
~~She gave me a good advice.~~

Uncountable and mass nouns cannot be made plural and cannot be used with *a* or *an*.

These common words are uncountable nouns in English, but refer to things that are considered countable in some other languages:

advice	homework	luggage	progress
baggage	information	machinery	research
furniture	knowledge	money	traffic

Here are some more common uncountable nouns that are often used incorrectly. Remember not to use *a* or *an* with them, and do not try to make them plural:

accommodation*	fun
equipment	housework
evidence	trouble
fruit	

*(uncountable in UK English, but in US English, you can say you are *looking for accommodations*)

A piece of advice, etc.

She gave me a piece of advice.

~~She gave me an advice.~~

How many items of baggage do you have?

~~How many baggages do you have?~~

If you want to talk about a particular amount of something that is expressed with an uncountable or a mass noun, you can put a quantity expression such as *a piece of*, *an item of*, or *a cup of* in front of the noun.

Do not put *a* or *an* in front of the word, or try to make it plural.

Here are some examples of quantity expressions with uncountable or mass nouns:

a piece of land   an item of clothing
a portion of rice   a piece of homework
a piece of paper   a piece of furniture
a drop of blood   a piece of information

Uncountable nouns ending in -s

I think that economics is interesting.   *His diabetes was getting worse.*
I think that economics are interesting.   *His diabetes were getting worse.*

Some uncountable nouns end in -s and look as if they are plural, although they are really singular. Do not put *a* or *an* in front of them, and make sure you use a singular verb, not a plural verb, with them.

Here are some uncountable nouns ending in -s:

aerobics	economics	mathematics	politics
athletics	electronics	measles	rabies
cards	genetics	mechanics	statistics
darts	gymnastics	mumps	
diabetes	linguistics	physics	

Plural nouns

She was wearing black trousers.   *The binoculars are in my bag.*
She was wearing a black trouser.   *The binoculars is in my bag.*

Some words for clothes and tools are plural in English, even though they are considered singular in some other languages. Do not miss the -s from the end of these words. Do not use *a* or *an* in front of them, and make sure you use a plural form of the verbs that you use with them.

Here are some common plural nouns for clothes and tools:

binoculars	pants/underpants	sunglasses
glasses	pyjamas	tights
jeans	scissors	trousers
knickers	shorts	tweezers

The police

My brother is a policeman.
My brother is a police.

I saw three police officers.
I saw three polices.

Note that *police* is a plural noun. You cannot use *a* or a number in front of it. To talk about a single person, use *policeman*, *policewoman*, or *police officer*. The plurals are *policemen*, *policewomen*, and *police officers*.

Collective nouns

Three of the crew were killed.
Three crew were killed.

I talked to a member of staff.
I talked to a staff.

Collective nouns refer to a group of people or things. You should not use *a*, *an* or a number in front of a collective noun when referring to a member or more than one member of that group. Instead, say something like: *four of the team/group*, etc., or *four members of the team/group*, etc.

Here is a list of some common collective nouns:

army	crew	government	staff
audience	enemy	group	team
committee	family	navy	
company	gang	public	

The government is *or* the government are?

The government has announced its decision.
The government has announced their decision.

The enemy are holding their position.
The enemy are holding its position.

The singular form of these nouns can be used with a singular or a plural verb in UK English. In US English, the singular form only is used:

*Our family **is**n't poor any more.* (UK and US)
*Our family **are**n't poor any more.* (UK)

If you use a pronoun to refer back to a collective noun, remember to make it singular if you have used a singular verb, and plural if you have used a plural verb.

Use of articles

A/an *or* the?

This is the house where he was born.
~~This is a house where he was born.~~

Where is the pen I was using?
~~Where is a pen I was using?~~

We use *the* to talk about a specific thing and *a* or *an* to talk about one of a set of things, when it is not important which specific one the thing is.

Compare the following:

*She wore **a dress**.*
***The dress** she wore was red.*

*I went to **a school** for girls.*
*I went to **the school** in my village.*

When to use an article

I have to take an exam.
~~I have to take exam.~~

Pollution is a serious problem.
~~The pollution is a serious problem.~~

You must always use *a*, *an*, or *the* (or a word such as *my*, *his*, etc.) before a singular countable noun:

*I bought **a computer**.*
*Would you like **an apple**?*
*Please close **the door**.*

When you use an uncountable noun or the plural form of a countable noun to talk about something in general, you do not use *a*, *an*, or *the*:

*They all live in big **houses**.*
*We all need **water** in order to live.*

However, if you are talking about a specific instance of something, you need to use *the* (or a word such as *my*, *his*, etc.) before a plural noun or an uncountable noun:

***The houses** in our street are all quite big.*
*I am grateful for **the advice** you gave me.*

School, hospital, prison, etc.

> Children here start school when they
>   are five.
> ~~Children here start the school when~~
>   ~~they are five.~~

> He was sentenced to a year in
>   prison.
> ~~He was sentenced to a year in the~~
>   ~~prison.~~

When you use words for institutions such as *church*, *college*, *hospital*, *prison*, *school*, and *university* in a general way, you do not use *the* in front of them. Only use *the* to talk about a specific place.

Compare the following:

> He was in **hospital** for several days.
> There was a fire at **the hospital**.

> Most of these students will go to **university**.
> **The university** is in the city centre.

The dentist, the supermarket, the theatre, etc.

> I have to go to the dentist this
>   afternoon.
> ~~I have to go to a dentist this afternoon.~~

> I bought this at the supermarket.
> ~~I bought this at a supermarket.~~

We use *the* before the names of places such as shops, medical institutions, or places of entertainment when we are talking about the place where we usually go.

Compare the following:

> I went to **the library** this morning.
> This town doesn't have **a library**.

> Shall we go to **the cinema** tonight?
> There is **a cinema** in the next town.

Breakfast, dinner, lunch, etc.

Let's play football after dinner. *Is it time for lunch yet?*
~~*Let's play football after the dinner.*~~ ~~*Is it time for the lunch yet?*~~

You do not use *the* before names of meals. However, if there is an adjective before the name of the meal, you must use *a* or *an*:

*We had **a delicious lunch** at Gemma's.*

The rich, the unemployed, etc.

The unemployed cannot afford this. *They give money to the poor.*
~~*The unemployeds cannot afford this.*~~ ~~*They give money to the poors.*~~

You can use *the* with words such as *rich*, *poor*, *young*, *old*, or *unemployed* to refer to all people of a particular type. When you use one of these words like this, do not add a plural *-s*.

Remember, though, that you must use a plural verb after these nouns.

Determiners and quantifiers

Some

Would you like a sandwich?
~~*Would you like some sandwich?*~~

Do you like oranges?
~~*Do you like some oranges?*~~

Some is used before plural countable nouns and uncountable nouns.
Do not use it before a singular countable noun.

Some is not used before plural countable nouns and uncountable nouns
to talk about things in general. In that case, nothing is needed before
the nouns.

Compare the following:

*If you have **children**, you will know what I mean.*
*I saw **some children** playing in the field.*

*They grow **rice** in their fields.*
*I had **some rice** with my meat.*

Some *or any?*

We don't have any food.
~~*We don't have some food.*~~

Do you have any children?
~~*Do you have some children?*~~

We usually use *some* in positive sentences and *any* in negative sentences:

*I saw **some people** outside.*
*I didn't see **any people** outside.*

You usually use *some* in questions about things that you know exist and *any*
in questions about whether something exists or not:

*Would you like **some soup**?*
*Do you have **any eggs**?*

Some *or some of,* any *or any of?*

Has any of this been helpful?
~~*Has any this been helpful?*~~

I'd like some of the cake.
~~*I'd like some the cake.*~~

Some and *any* can be used directly before a noun, but if you use them before a noun phrase beginning with *the, this, these, that, those,* or a word such as *my* or *your,* you must use *some of* or *any of.*

Much *or* many?

How many eggs do we need?
~~How much eggs do we need?~~

She gave me too much rice.
~~She gave me too many rice.~~

You use *many* in front of plural countable nouns, and *much* in front of uncountable nouns.

Much, many, *or* a lot of?

We ate a lot of food.

~~We ate much food.~~

This book will give you a lot of information.
~~This book will give you much information.~~

Much is not usually used in front of uncountable nouns in statements. It is more common to use *a lot of.*

Many is more common in statements than *much*:

He had **many friends**.
I applied for **many jobs**.

However, it is still slightly formal, and *a lot of* is more common.

Little *or* not much?

There isn't much food left.
~~There is little food left.~~

I don't have much work to do.
~~I have little work to do.~~

Little can be used before uncountable nouns, but it is rather formal:

We've made **little** progress.

It is much more common to use *not much* instead:

We have**n't** made **much** progress.

However, if you want to emphasize how little of something there is, you can use *very little*:

We have **very little** time left.

A little, a few, or a bit of?

I ate a few chips and peas.
~~I ate a little chips and peas.~~

Let's have a bit of fun!
~~Let's have a little fun!~~

You use *a little* in front of uncountable nouns and *a few* in front of plural countable nouns. However, *a little* is rather formal, so in speech and informal writing, it is more common to say *a bit of*.

Little or a little?

Would you like a little milk in your tea?

~~Would you like little milk in your tea?~~

I hope to make a little progress today.

~~I hope to make little progress today.~~

Little and *a little* are both used in front of nouns, but they do not have the same meaning. You use *a little* to show that you are talking about a small amount or quantity of something. When you use *little*, you are emphasizing that there is only a small amount or quantity of something.

Compare the following:

Sam had made a little progress.
Sam had made little progress.

The first sentence is more positive, saying that Sam had made progress, even if it was not a large amount. The second sentence is more negative, emphasizing that the amount of progress was very small.

Few or a few?

I invited a few friends.

~~I invited few friends.~~

Here are a few ideas that might help you.
~~Here are few ideas that might help you.~~

Few and *a few* are both used in front of nouns, but they do not have the same meaning. You use *a few* to show that you are talking about a small number of people or things.

Few without *a* is much less common. It is used to emphasize that there are only a small number of people or things. Compare the following:

> *Maria has **a few** friends in the city.*
> *Maria has **few** friends in the city.*

The first sentence is more positive, saying that although Maria doesn't have a lot of friends in the city, she does have some. The second sentence is more negative, emphasizing the fact that Maria does not have many friends there.

Note that in conversation and in less formal writing, it is very unusual to use *few* on its own. It is much more common to say *not many*:

> *They haven't got **many** books.*
> *I don't have **many** visitors.*

A lot *or* a lot of?

> *A lot of people thought it was funny.*   *It costs a lot of money.*
> *A lot people thought it was funny.*   *It costs a lot money.*

If you use *a lot* or *lots* before a noun, you must always use *of*.

Another *or* other?

> *They arrange things better in other*   *Let's choose another song.*
> *countries.*
> *They arrange things better in another*   *Let's choose other song.*
> *countries.*

Another means 'one other'. Do not use it in front of a plural noun. You use *other* in front of a plural noun to talk about things or people that are different from the ones you have just mentioned.

Both, most, many of the ...

> *Both of the boys were Hungarian.*   *Most people had gone home.*
> *Both of boys were Hungarian.*   *Most the people had gone home.*

Both, *most*, and *many* are used directly in front of plural nouns; but you must use *of* in front of a phrase beginning with *the*, *this*, *that*, or a word such as *him*, *their*, etc.

Both is also used directly before two nouns linked with *and*:

> **Both she and the baby** were safe.
> I told **both Richard and George**.

All *or* every?

> I go to school *every day*.   *Every* child in the school got a present.
> ~~I go to school all the days.~~   ~~All child in the school got a present.~~

Every has a similar meaning to *all*, but *every* is used in front of a singular noun, while *all* is used in front of a plural noun.

However, there is a difference between *every* and *all* when you use them with expressions of time. For example, if you spend *all day* doing something, you spend the whole of the day doing it. If you do something *every day*, you keep doing it each day.

Each *or* every?

> Nearly *every* person received a prize.   Not *every* chair is broken.
> ~~Nearly each person received a prize.~~   ~~Not each chair is broken.~~

You cannot use words such as *nearly*, *almost*, or *not* in front of *each*, but you can use them in front of *every*.

Every/each + singular verb

> *Every* child *has* a seat.   *Each* day *is* the same.
> ~~Every child have a seat.~~   ~~Each day are the same.~~

After *every/each* + noun, you use a singular verb.

Note that in modern English, it is acceptable to refer back using the third person plural pronoun:

> **Each** student has **their** own desk.
> **Every** person knew what **they** had to do.

Either *and* neither, either of *and* neither of

> *Either parent can give permission.*
> ~~*Either parents can give permission.*~~

> *Neither of the hotels was suitable.*
> ~~*Neither the hotels was suitable.*~~

Either and *neither* are used in front of a singular countable noun, and the verb must be singular.

Either of and *neither of* are used in front of a plural pronoun or in front of a plural countable noun if followed by a word such as *the*, *this*, *my*, etc. It is not correct to omit *of*.

In formal English, the verb that follows *either/neither of* + plural noun must be singular, although in speech people often use a plural verb.

None of

> *None of them were ready.*
> ~~*None of them weren't ready.*~~

> *I didn't want any of them.*
> ~~*I didn't want none of them.*~~

You do not usually use any other negative word after *none of*.

Do not use *none of* as the object of a sentence that already has a negative word in it.

You can use a singular or a plural verb after *none of*. Using a singular verb sounds slightly more formal:

> **None of** the boys **has** a coat.
> **None of** the boys **have** a coat.

Remember that you only use *none of* to talk about a group of three or more things or people. If you want to talk about two things or people, use *neither of* or *neither*.

No one, nobody, *or* none of?

> *None of the children could speak French.*
> ~~*No one of the children could speak French.*~~

> *None of us knew the answer.*
> ~~*Nobody of us knew the answer.*~~

Do not use *of* after *no one* or *nobody*. If you want to make a negative sentence about all the members of a group, use *none of*.

Each (of) *or* none of?

None of the boys enjoyed football.	*None of them are African.*
~~Each boy did not enjoy football.~~	~~Each of them is not African.~~

Do not use *each* or *each of* in a negative sentence. Use *none of* instead.

This, that, these, and those

I'd like some of these apples.	*Look at that bird over there.*
~~I'd like some of this apples.~~	~~Look at this bird over there.~~

This and *that* are used before singular nouns and uncountable nouns.
These and *those* are used in front of plural countable nouns.

This and *these* are used for things that are close to you, while *that* and *those* are used for things that you can see but which are further away.

Enough *or* not enough?

Not enough people came.	*We didn't collect enough money.*
~~Enough people didn't come.~~	~~Enough money wasn't collected.~~

Do not use *enough* and a noun as the subject of a negative sentence. Either use *not enough*, or make a sentence in which the noun after *enough* is the object of the negative sentence.

Such

She is such a nice woman.	*You've had such bad luck.*
~~She is a such nice woman.~~	~~You've had such a bad luck.~~

You use *such a* or *such an* in front of a singular noun. Do not leave out *a* or *an*. However, before a plural noun or an uncountable noun, you use *such* on its own.

Prepositions and verb patterns

Prepositions after nouns

I hate his dependence on me.

~~I hate his dependence of me.~~

There has been a decrease in their wages.

~~There has been a decrease of their wages.~~

It is important to use the correct preposition after a noun. A good dictionary will tell you which preposition to use.

Note the following noun + prepositions, which are often used incorrectly:

I don't know the **answer to** your question. (Not ~~of~~)
What is the **cause of** the problem? (Not ~~for~~)
I'm doing a **course in** electronics. (Not ~~of~~)
Make sure you pay **attention to** what he tells you. (Not ~~at~~)
The **reason for** the delay was not explained. (Not ~~of~~)

Nouns + to- infinitive

We have the freedom to do what we like.

~~We have the freedom of doing what we like.~~

I admired her ability to make friends.

~~I admired her ability of making friends.~~

Some nouns are often followed by a to- infinitive. You should not use a preposition + -ing verb instead.

Here are some more nouns that are followed by a to- infinitive and cannot be used with of + -ing verb:

desire	hurry	reason	right
failure	inability	refusal	wish
haste	permission	request	

Nouns + preposition + -*ing* verb

There is no possibility of going there.   *I have no intention of telling him.*
~~There is no possibility to go there.~~   ~~I have no intention to tell him.~~

When you use a preposition after a noun, the verb that follows must be in the -*ing* form.

Look at the following examples:

*That is the **advantage of having** a job.*
*We have no **chance of winning**.*
*We had **difficulty in making** him understand.*
*This had the **effect of making** him very angry.*

Plurals

One glass, two glasses

We put the books into boxes.
~~We put the books into boxs.~~

I bought a box of matches.
~~I bought a box of match's.~~

You use the plural -*es* for nouns that end in -*sh*, -*ch*, -*ss*, -*x*, or -*s*.

You should never use -'*s* to make a plural.

One country, two countries

There were some ladies on the bus.

~~There were some ladys on the bus.~~

We had lots of opportunities to talk.

~~We had lots of opportunity's to talk.~~

For nouns which end in a consonant + -*y*, you usually form the plural by changing -*y* to -*ies*.

One knife, two knives

The leaves are turning yellow.
~~The leafs are turning yellow.~~

We put up some shelves.
~~We put up some shelfs.~~

There are a few nouns ending in -*f* or -*fe* where you form the plural by changing -*f*/-*fe* to -*ves*.

Here is a list of some common ones:

calf	leaf	scarf	wife
half	life	shelf	wolf
knife	loaf	thief	

One tomato, two tomatoes

All my heroes are sportspeople.
~~All my heros are sportspeople.~~

I'd like some potatoes.
~~I'd like some potato's.~~

With many nouns that end in -*o*, you just add -*s* to form the plural. However, some words like *echo*, *hero*, *potato*, and *tomato* form their plurals with -*es*.

Irregular plurals

We played with the children.
~~We played with the childs.~~

My teeth hurt.
~~My tooths hurt.~~

The following common nouns have irregular plurals:

aircraft → aircraft
child → children
crisis → crises
foot → feet
goose → geese

man → men
mouse → mice
tooth → teeth
woman → women
ox → oxen

Note that *people* is the normal plural of *person*. *Persons* is sometimes used in formal documents.

Adjectives

Position of adjectives

Adjectives that never go before nouns

I tried to comfort the frightened boy.

~~I tried to comfort the afraid boy.~~

I spoke to the teacher. She was obviously sorry.

~~I spoke to the sorry teacher.~~

Some adjectives are normally used only after a linking verb and not in front of a noun. Here is a list of some of these adjectives.

afraid	awake	ill	sure
alive	aware	likely	unable
alone	content	ready	unlikely
apart	due	safe	well
asleep	glad	sorry	

Often an adjective with a very similar meaning can be used in front of a noun.

Compare the following:

The baby was **asleep**.
I looked at the **sleeping** baby.

Order of adjectives

She has a sweet little girl.
~~She has a little sweet girl.~~

They have a nice big house.
~~They have a big nice house.~~

In a list of adjectives, the subjective adjective that shows your opinion usually comes first.

Comparing adjectives

-Er/-est *or* more/most?

My brother is older than me.
~~My brother is more old than me.~~

She's the most beautiful girl in my class.
~~She's the beautifulest girl in my class.~~

With adjectives that have one syllable, to form a comparative or superlative, you usually add -er or -est to the end:

*It's **colder** today than yesterday.*
*John is one of the **nicest** people I've ever met.*

Adjectives with three or more syllables usually have comparatives or superlatives with *more* or *most*:

*Driving is **more dangerous** than flying.*
*That's the **most ridiculous** thing I've ever heard.*

For most adjectives that have two syllables, you can either use -er/-est or more/most. However, for adjectives with two syllables ending in -y, you use -er/-est:

*I was **luckier** this time.*
*She looks **prettier** with short hair.*

Note that you only use -er/-est or more/most. Do not try to use both. It is not correct to say ~~She's more prettier than her sister.~~

Hotter, hottest/bigger, biggest, etc.

It's hotter in July.
~~It's hoter in July.~~

It's the wettest day of the year.
~~It's the wetest day of the year.~~

If an adjective with one syllable ends in a single vowel followed by a single consonant, you double the consonant when adding an -er or -est.

Irregular comparatives + superlatives

This course is better than the last one.
~~This course is more good than the last one.~~

Tom's house is furthest from here.
~~Tom's house is farest from here.~~

Good, *bad*, and *far* have special comparatives and superlatives:

good → better → best
bad → worse → worst
far → further → furthest

Note that the usual comparative form of *ill* is *worse*:

*The next day I felt **worse**.*

A bit/a lot/much, etc. hotter

It's a bit hotter today.
It's quite hotter today.

This restaurant is much nicer.
This restaurant is really nicer.

Adverbs which are often used in front of adjectives, such as *quite*, *rather*, and *very*, are not used in front of comparative forms. Instead, you should use a word or phrase such as *a bit*, *a lot*, or *much*.

Newer/better/worse, etc. than ...

My phone's newer than yours.
My phone's newer as yours.

Coffee is more expensive than tea.
Coffee is more expensive as tea.

You use *than* after comparative adjectives. Do not use *as*.

As good/bad, etc. as ...

He's as tall as Dan.
He's as tall like Dan.

Her house isn't as nice as Maria's.
Her house isn't as nice than Maria's.

You use *as ... as* to say that two people, things, or amounts are the same. Do not use *like* or *than* instead of the second *as*.

Equally good/bad, etc.

This restaurant is equally good.
This restaurant is equally as good.

She's just as clever as him.
She's equally as clever as him.

Equally is followed by an adjective on its own. Do not use *as* after *equally*. If you want to mention two things in one sentence, use *just as ... as* instead.

Expressing degree with adjectives

Very *or* absolutely?

> It was absolutely freezing.
> ~~It was absolutely cold.~~

> The food was absolutely terrible.
> ~~The food was absolutely bad.~~

You use *very* to emphasize most adjectives, but you cannot use *very* with adjectives which already describe an extreme quality. Do not say, for example, that something is ~~very enormous~~. Instead, say that something is *absolutely enormous*. Compare these sentences:

> It was **very** hot.
> It was **absolutely** boiling.

> James was **very** angry.
> James was **absolutely** furious.

> His wife was **very** pretty.
> His wife was **absolutely** beautiful.

Here is a list of extreme adjectives that you must put *absolutely* before if you want to emphasize them:

appalling	essential	massive	vast
awful	excellent	perfect	wonderful
brilliant	fantastic	superb	
dreadful	furious	terrible	
enormous	huge	unique	

Quite, rather, a bit, etc.

> He's quite short.
> ~~He's quite short man.~~

> The room is a bit small.
> ~~It's a bit small room.~~

Words and phrases meaning 'to a small degree', such as *quite*, *rather*, *slightly*, and *a bit*, are frequently put before adjectives. Do not, however, use them before adjectives that are in front of nouns unless you add an article before the adjective (eg *quite a*) and *of* in the case of *a bit* (eg *a bit of a*).

Too hot/tired/poor, etc.

It's too hot to play football.

~~It's too much hot to play football.~~

I can't go out tonight. I'm much too tired.

~~I can't go out tonight. I'm too much tired.~~

Do not use *too much* or *much too much* in front of an adjective which is not followed by a noun. Simply say *too hot/tired/poor*, etc. or, to make this more extreme, *far* or *much too hot/tired/poor*, etc.

Enough

He's not clever enough.

~~He's not enough clever.~~

Are the bananas ripe enough to eat?

~~Are the bananas ripe enough that we can eat them?~~

When you are using *enough* with an adjective to say that someone or something has as much of a quality as is needed, use *enough* after the adjective. Also, do not use a *that-* clause after *enough* when you are saying what is needed for something to be possible. Instead, use *to-* infinitive:

*I'm not strong enough **to lift** them.*
*Are you brave enough **to do** it?*

-ing and *-ed* adjectives

Shocked *or* shocking?

We were very shocked by the news.
~~*We were very shocking by the news.*~~

His classes are so boring!
~~*His classes are so bored!*~~

Be careful. There are a number of adjectives, such as *bored* and *boring*, that deal with the same emotion or quality, (and start with the same letters), but that are very different in meaning. Adjectives ending in *-ing* describe a quality in something that can affect you in a particular way. Adjectives ending in *-ed* describe you when you are affected by this particular quality. Compare the following sentences:

*It was surpris**ing** that she left so suddenly.*
*We were very surpris**ed** when she left so suddenly.*

*I found Ava's comments very interest**ing**.*
*I was very interest**ed** in Ava's comments.*

*She's a very charm**ing** little girl.*
*We were all charm**ed** by her.*

Prepositions after adjectives

Choosing the right preposition

We're all responsible for cleaning our own rooms.
~~We're all responsible to clean our own rooms.~~

Several reporters were present at the event.
~~Several reporters were present in the event.~~

Some adjectives are followed by a particular preposition when they are used after a linking verb, and it is important to use the right one.

Here are some important adjective + preposition combinations:

accustomed to	fond of
adjacent to	full of
allergic to	incapable of
averse to	interested in
aware of	lacking in
capable of	prone to
close to	related to
compatible with	resigned to
devoted to	resistant to
different from	similar to
excited about	susceptible to
filled with	

In some cases, there is a choice between two prepositions after the adjective. Here are some adjectives that are used with either of two prepositions:

connected to/with	inclined to/towards
dependent on/upon	parallel to/with
immune from/to	reliant on/upon

Note also that British speakers of English sometimes say that one thing is *different to* another thing, meaning the same as *different from*. Some people consider *different to* incorrect so in formal writing, it is better to use *different from*.

Structures after adjectives

Adjective + *to-* infinitive

Unfortunately, we're unable to help on
  the day.
~~Unfortunately, we're unable.~~

He's bound to say yes.

~~He's bound.~~

Some adjectives are always followed by a *to-* infinitive when they come
after a linking verb. Here is a list of adjectives that behave like this:

able	inclined	unable
bound	liable	unwilling
due	likely	willing

Note that you can also use a clause beginning with a *to-* infinitive after
many other adjectives to give more information about something. Look at
the following examples:

*I was afraid **to go** home.*
*I was embarrassed **to tell** her.*
*We were so happy **to see** her.*
*The instructions were very easy **to follow**.*

Note also that if you use the adjective *anxious*, meaning 'very keen to do
something', you need to follow it with a *to-* infinitive:

*We were anxious **to leave**.*

Adjective + *that-* clause

She was worried that she might be late.

~~She was worried to be late.~~

Are you confident that you will
  win?

~~Are you confident to win?~~

A *that-* clause is often used after adjectives linking someone's feelings or
beliefs and the thing that they relate to. These adjectives often have a *that-*
clause after them:

afraid	ashamed	confident
amazed	astonished	conscious
angry	aware	convinced
annoyed	certain	definite
anxious	concerned	determined

disappointed
disgusted
fortunate
frightened
furious
glad
grateful
happy
horrified
lucky

optimistic
pessimistic
pleased
positive
proud
puzzled
relieved
sad
satisfied
scared

shocked
sorry
sure
surprised
suspicious
terrified
unaware
worried

Determiner + adjective + noun/*one*

The pink/small/cheap, etc. one

I like them all, but best of all, I like the blue one.

~~*I like them all, but best of all, I like the blue.*~~

It was nice, but not as nice as the wooden one.

~~*It was nice, but not as nice as the wooden.*~~

If an adjective is used after a determiner, it must be followed by a noun or *one*.

Adverbs and Adverbial Phrases

How to use adverbs and adverbial phrases

Adverb, not adjective

She sings very well.
~~She sings very good.~~

James speaks very quickly.
~~James speaks very quick.~~

If you want to say how someone does something, or how something happens, you need to use an adverb and not an adjective. Adverbs in English are often formed from an adjective plus -ly:

I was just sitting there **quietly**, reading my book.
I thought he didn't do too **badly**.
Could you speak more **slowly**, please?
He very **carefully** laid the baby down on the bed.

Adverbs that look like adjectives (hard, fast, late, etc.)

They ran fast.

~~They ran fastly.~~

We've all worked so hard on this
  project.

~~We've all worked so hardly on this
  project.~~

Be careful. Some adverbs of manner are irregular, having the same form as the adjective. These examples show a group of the most common adverbs that are the same as the adjectives:

Take two tablets three times **daily**.
You can fly **direct** to Barcelona from Dublin airport.
We set off **early**.
How **far** can you run?
You drive too **fast**.
We've had a few problems but basically, we're doing **fine**. (Informal)
Dan works really **hard**.
Harrison can jump really **high**.
Unfortunately, we arrived **late**.
Planes fly quite **low** over this area.

Well, *not* good

I thought you did that really well.
~~I thought you did that really good.~~

She swam really well.
~~She swam really goodly.~~

Remember that the very common adverb from *good* is *well*. The adverb from *bad*, however, is *badly*:

She sings really **well**.
She sings really **badly**.

Barely, hardly, rarely, scarcely, seldom

I've hardly seen you today!
~~I haven't hardly seen you today!~~

She barely ate anything.
~~She barely ate nothing.~~

The adverbs *barely*, *hardly*, *rarely*, *scarcely*, and *seldom* ('broad negatives') are used to make a statement almost negative. Do not use broad negatives with *not* and do not use another negative word, such as *nothing* or *no one*:

I **seldom** eat breakfast.
Karl **rarely** says anything in meetings.
I **scarcely** had time to speak to anyone.

If you use an auxiliary verb or modal verb with a broad negative, put the auxiliary verb or modal verb first. Say, for example, *He can **barely** read*. Do not say ~~He barely can read.~~

Barely/hardly/scarcely ... when

We had hardly finished eating when
   James arrived.
~~We had hardly finished eating than
   James arrived.~~

The film had scarcely started when
   Josie burst into tears.
~~The film had scarcely started than
   Josie burst into tears.~~

The adverbs *barely*, *hardly*, and *scarcely* are sometimes used in longer structures, to say that one thing happened immediately after another. In structures like these, use *when* in the second part of the sentence, and not *than*.

After all *or* finally/lastly?

Finally, I want to thank you all for coming.
~~*After all, I want to thank you all for coming.*~~

Lastly, remember to bring your sports kits with you tomorrow.
~~*After all, remember to bring your sports kits with you tomorrow.*~~

Do not use *after all* to introduce a final point, question, or topic. Instead, use *finally* or *lastly*.

First *or* firstly?

Rachel spoke first.
~~*Rachel spoke firstly.*~~

Which task should we do first?
~~*Which task should we do firstly?*~~

Do not use *firstly* to mean 'before anyone or anything else'. The adverb here is *first*.

Note also that the phrase ~~*firstly of all*~~ does not exist. The phrase is *first of all*:

First of all, *I'd like to introduce myself.*

You can use *first* or *firstly* to introduce the first point in a discussion:

First/firstly, *I'd like to welcome Mona to our meeting.*

Long

I've known Al for a long time.
~~*I've known Al long.*~~

I can't stay long.
~~*It's okay – I can stay long.*~~

The adverb *long* is normally used only in questions and negative sentences:

*How **long** have you known Al?*
*We can't stay **long**.*

It is not usually used in positive statements. For positive statements, use *a long time*:

*I've lived here for **a long time**.*
*I spent **a long time** in the library.*

Downstairs/upstairs

I ran downstairs to answer the door.
~~I ran to downstairs to answer the door.~~

I tripped as I was going upstairs.
~~I tripped as I was going to upstairs.~~

Do not use the preposition *to* before the adverbs *downstairs* and *upstairs*.

Here

Come here, Liam.

~~Come to here, Liam.~~

It'll take them an hour or more to drive here.

~~It'll take them an hour or more to drive to here.~~

Remember that *to* is never used before *here*.

Often

I kept calling her.

~~I called her often yesterday.~~

In the meeting I asked him several times to explain what he meant.

~~In the meeting I often asked him to explain what he meant.~~

Often is not used to mean 'several times over a short period'. For this meaning, use phrases such as *to keep doing* something or to do something *several times* or *a number of times*:

I **kept shouting** his name but he couldn't hear me.
I reminded you **several times** last week to take that book back.
I've asked Lucy to reply **a number of times**.

Never

He never writes to me.
~~He does never write to me.~~

He never says anything.
~~He never says nothing.~~

Do not use *do* in front of *never*. Do not use another negative word with *never*. For example, do not say ~~I haven't never been there~~ or ~~I never said nothing~~. Instead, say *I have never been there* and *I never said anything*.

I've **never** seen anything so funny in my life.
I'd **never** seen anyone so thin.
It was an experience I'll **never** forget.

Quite

It was quite a cold day.

~~It was a quite cold day.~~

The train is slightly quicker than the bus.

~~The train is quite quicker than the bus.~~

You can use the adverb *quite* (meaning 'slightly') in front of a structure which consists of *a*, an adjective, and then a noun. For example, instead of saying *He was quite tall*, you can say *He was quite a tall man*. In sentences like these, you put *quite* in front of *a*, not after it:

It was **quite an** odd thing to say.

Do not use *quite* in front of comparative adjectives and adverbs. Do not say, for example, ~~William is quite taller than his brother~~. Instead, use *a bit*, *a little*, or *slightly*:

William is **slightly** taller than his brother.
We arrived **a little** earlier than expected.
The jacket is **a bit** darker than the trousers.

Too

It's (much) too hot to play football.

~~It's too much hot to play football.~~

These boots are too big.

~~These are too big boots.~~

Do not use *too much* or *much too much* in front of an adjective. You do not usually use *too* with an adjective that is in front of a noun.

As soon as

He left as soon as we arrived.

~~He left as soon we arrived.~~

As soon as Cara's ready, we can go.

~~As soon Cara's ready, we can go.~~

You use the phrase *as soon as* to say that one event happens immediately after another. Do not leave out the second *as*.

As well

He plays football as well as tennis.
He plays football as well tennis.

I saw Dan and I saw Ben as well.
I saw Dan and as well I saw Ben.

You use the phrase *as well as* + noun to mean 'in addition to'. Do not leave out the second *as*. When you use *as well* to add further information about something, you put it at the end of the sentence, not before the second part of the sentence.

I'd/you'd, etc. better ...

I'd better call my dad.
I better call my dad.

They'd better leave now.
They'd better to leave now.

If you say that someone *had better* do something, you mean that they ought to do it. *Had better* is always followed by an infinitive without *to*. People usually shorten *had* to -'d. Do not leave out -'d.

Very much

I like your parents very much.
I like very much your parents.

I enjoyed the opera very much.
I enjoyed very much the opera.

Do not use *very much* before the object of the sentence. Use it at the end of the sentence. Note that *very much* is rather formal. It is more common to use *a lot* or *really*:

I **really** enjoyed the opera.
I like your parents **a lot**.

Position of adverbs and adverbial phrases

Adverbs of frequency

I never go to the theatre.
Never I go to the theatre.

I always see Carlo in this café.
I see always Carlo in this café.

The adverbs *always* and *never* always go in front of the verb, unless the verb is *be*. If the verb is *be*, the adverb usually goes after it:

*Rebecca **always** dresses beautifully.*
*Rebecca is **never** on time.*
*I **always** buy the same brand of toothpaste.*
*I'm **never** cross with her about it.*

If you are using an auxiliary verb or modal, you put *always* and *never* after it and not before it:

*I have **always** driven this way.*
*We may **never** know what happened to him.*

Note that the usual place for other adverbs of frequency (*sometimes*, *often*, *usually*, etc.) is in front of the verb, though these adverbs are sometimes used at the start or end of a sentence:

*I **often** go to the park at lunch.*
***Often**, I go to the park at lunch.*
*I **sometimes** go there after work.*
*I go there after work **sometimes**.*

Almost, nearly, really, etc.

He almost got there.
He got there almost.

I really enjoyed working with him.
Really I enjoyed working with him.

The adverbs of degree *almost, largely, nearly, really,* and *virtually* are nearly always used in front of the main verb. They are very rarely used at the beginning or the end of a clause:

*We **almost** finished the work.*
*He **nearly** died in the accident.*
*She **virtually** admitted that it was her fault.*
*Conflict has **largely** disappeared in the region.*

Note that *almost* and *nearly* only go before nouns after the verb *be*. You cannot say ~~We got there at almost 5 o'clock.~~, but you can say *It was almost 5 o'clock when we got there*.

Adverbial phrases and objects

> *I see Lucy a lot.*
> ~~I see a lot Lucy.~~

> *I like their new record a lot.*
> ~~I like a lot their new record.~~

An adverbial phrase (a group of words which functions as an adverb) does not generally come between a verb and its object:

> *I like Julia **a great deal**.*
> *We cook them **a lot** at home.*
> *We eat bread **all the time**.*

Adverbs of manner

> *She listened carefully.*
> ~~She carefully listened.~~

> *Andrew laughed loudly.*
> ~~Andrew loudly laughed.~~

If a sentence only consists of a subject, a verb, and an adverb of manner, the adverb usually comes at the end. It is rarely put in front of the verb.

Comparing adverbs

Adverb, not adjective

He walks more slowly than me.
~~He walks slower than me.~~

I eat more quickly than you.
~~I eat quicker than you.~~

Remember that, with adverbs ending in -ly or adverbs of two or more syllables, you must use more or most plus the adverb to form the comparative or superlative:

Cassidy certainly spoke **more impressively** than her rivals.
I was dressed **more casually** than anyone else there.
Of all of the children, Ethan waited the **most patiently**.

Better, worse, etc.

Some of the group could ski better than others.
~~Some of the group could ski more well than others.~~

We played worse than in our previous match.
~~We played more badly than in our previous match.~~

Remember that the comparative and superlative forms of well and badly are better/best and worse/worst:

I changed seats so that I could see **better**.
Use whatever method works **best** for you.
If anything, I swim **worse** now than I did when I was a child.
The south of England was the **worst** affected area.

Pronouns

Personal pronouns

I, he, they, etc.

My mother wants to speak to you.

~~*My mother she wants to speak to you.*~~

The green chairs are very uncomfortable.

~~*The green chairs they are very uncomfortable.*~~

You use a pronoun instead of a noun or a noun phrase. Do not use a pronoun in addition to a noun or a noun phrase.

He *or* him, we *or* us, etc.?

I like her.
~~*I like she.*~~

The teacher told us to be quiet.
~~*The teacher told we to be quiet.*~~

The following are object pronouns: *me*, *you*, *him*, *her*, *it*, *us*, and *them*.

When the noun or noun phrase you want to replace is the object of the sentence, you use these pronouns.

When the noun or noun phrase you want to replace is the subject of the sentence, you use *I*, *you*, *he*, *she*, *it*, *we*, or *they*.

Me *or* I?

'Who is it?' – 'It's me.'
~~*'Who is it?' – 'It's I.'*~~

'Who called?' – 'Me.'
~~*'Who called?' – 'I.'*~~

In modern English, you do not use *I* after the verb *be*. You also do not use *I* as a single-word answer to a question.

My friend and I

My friend and I went shopping.

~~*Me and my friend went shopping.*~~

Mum and I had a good talk about it.

~~*Me and Mum had a good talk about it.*~~

Although you may hear people say things like *Me and my friend went shopping* in very informal speech, this use is not considered correct, and should never be written.

The best way to decide whether to use *me* or *I* when you are talking about you and someone else is to think about which pronoun you would use if you were talking just about you.

For example, look at the following:

> *I like dancing.*
> *Ella and I like dancing.*
>
> *Rob gave **me** some sweets.*
> *Rob gave Max and **me** some sweets.*

They *or* he/she?

> *Does everyone have the books **they** need?*
> *Does everyone have the books **he or she** needs?*

In modern English, it is common and acceptable to use *they* in order to avoid saying *he* or *she*. It is not wrong to say *he* or *she*, but it sounds very formal and old-fashioned.

If you use *they* like this, remember to use a plural verb after it.

You can use *their* in the same way, to avoid saying *his* or *her*:

> *Every student must study hard for **their** exams.*

If you are writing something extremely formal, you may prefer to make the subject of the sentence plural:

> *All of the students must study hard for **their** exams.*

Possessive pronouns

Mine, yours, theirs, etc.

Is this book hers?
Is this the book of her?

That is its lid.
That lid is its.

Possessive pronouns show who the person or thing you are referring to belongs to or is connected with.

The possessive pronouns are *mine*, *yours*, *his*, *hers*, *ours*, and *theirs*.

Note that there is no possessive pronoun for *it*.

Reflexive pronouns

Myself, yourself, herself, etc.

> I bought myself a new watch.
> ~~I bought me a new watch.~~

> He got himself a drink.
> ~~He got him a drink.~~

Reflexive pronouns are used as the object of a verb or preposition when the person or thing affected by an action is the same as the person or thing doing it. Do not use an object pronoun instead.

The reflexive pronouns are *myself*, *yourself*, *himself*, *herself*, *itself*, *ourselves*, *yourselves*, and *themselves*.

Make sure you spell these reflexive pronouns correctly. Do not write ~~hisself~~ or ~~youself~~.

Other types of pronoun

Relative pronouns

For information on relative pronouns, see 'Relative clauses' in the section 'Sentences'.

Wh- pronouns

For information on *wh-* pronouns, see 'Questions' in the section 'Sentences'.

Anyone, no one, etc.

Everyone knows her.
~~Everyone know her.~~

Has anyone seen my book?
~~Have anyone seen my book?~~

Indefinite pronouns are used to refer to people or things without saying exactly who or what they are. You always use singular verbs with them. However, in modern English, it is acceptable to use a plural pronoun to refer back:

*Has **everyone** got **their** passport?*
*Has **anyone** got an umbrella **they** can lend me?*

The indefinite pronouns are:

anybody	everyone	nothing
anyone	everything	somebody
anything	nobody	someone
everybody	no one (or no-one)	something

Anyone *or* any one?

Did you meet anyone on the way?
~~Did you meet any one on the way?~~

I don't know anything about it.
~~I don't know any thing about it.~~

With the exception of *no one*, the indefinite pronouns must always be written as one word.

Someone, somebody, or anyone?

I don't know anyone in New York.
I don't know somebody in New York.

I don't think anyone likes this song.
I don't think someone likes this song.

You do not usually use *someone* or *somebody* as part of the object of a negative sentence. Use *anyone* instead.

Someone, somebody, or one of?

One of my friends is an artist.
Someone of my friends is an artist.

I'll ask one of my teachers.
I'll ask somebody of my teachers.

Do not use *someone* or *somebody* with *of* in front of the plural form of a noun. Use *one of* instead.

Something or anything?

We haven't had anything to eat.
We haven't had something to eat.

I didn't say anything.
I didn't say something.

You do not usually use *something* as part of the object of a negative sentence. Use *anything* instead.

All or everything/everyone?

I don't understand everything.
I don't understand all.

I gave everyone a pen.
I gave all a pen.

Do not use *all* on its own like this. If you want to use *all*, it must be used before *of* or after a word such as *them* or *us*:

*I don't know **all of** the people here.*
*I managed to speak to them **all**.*

Nobody, no one, nothing, nowhere, *and* none

Nobody came to the party.
Nobody didn't come to the party.

I couldn't find him anywhere.
I couldn't find him nowhere.

Do not use any other negative word after *nobody*, *no one*, *nothing*, *nowhere*, or *none*.

Do not use these words as the object of a sentence that already has a negative word in it. Use a positive word such as *anyone* or *anywhere* instead.

This, that, these, *and* those

You wanted apples, Madam. Would you like these here?
You wanted apples, Madam. Would you like this here?

How much is that over there?

How much is this over there?

This and *that* are used to replace singular nouns and uncountable nouns. *These* and *those* are used to replace plural countable nouns.

This and *these* are used for things that are close to you, while *that* and *those* are used for things that you can see but which are further away.

There is *or* it is?

There is a lot of traffic.
It is a lot of traffic.

It is four days since she arrived.
There are four days since she arrived.

When you are talking about something being present or existing, use *there is* or *there are*. Do not try to form the sentence with *it is* or *they are*.

Do not use *there is* or *there are* with *since* to say how long ago something happened. Use *it is* or *it's* instead.

Some *or* any?

He asked for money but I didn't have any.
He asked for money but I didn't have some.

I need some sugar. Do you have any?

I need some sugar. Do you have some?

We usually use *some* in positive sentences and *any* in negative sentences.

> *There's plenty of milk – I bought **some** yesterday.*
> *I wanted to get mangoes, but the shop didn't have **any**.*

You usually use *some* in questions about things that you know exist and *any* in questions about whether something exists or not:

> *I've made soup – would you like **some**?*
> *I love children. Do you have **any**?*

Some, one, *or* ones?

> *If you like grapes, I'll get you some.*   *If you want a cake, just take one.*
> ~~If you like grapes, I'll get you ones.~~   ~~If you want a cake, just take some.~~

In positive sentences, use *some* to replace a plural noun or an uncountable noun, and *one* to replace a single countable noun.

Note that after a word such as *the* or *this*, you use *one* for a singular countable noun and *ones* for a plural countable noun:

> *Which biscuit do you want ... this **one**?*
> *Of all the flowers, I like these **ones** best.*

Much *or* many?

> *I'll get the eggs. How many do we need?*   *I like soup, but he gave me too much.*
> ~~I'll get the eggs. How much do we need?~~   ~~I like soup, but he gave me too many.~~

You use *many* to replace plural countable nouns, and *much* to replace uncountable nouns.

Much *or* a lot?

> *I ate a lot last night.*   *He knows a lot about butterflies.*
> ~~I ate much last night.~~   ~~He knows much about butterflies.~~

You do not usually use *much* as an object pronoun in positive sentences. Instead, use *a lot*.

Little *or* a little?

> 'Did you make any progress?' – 'Yes, a little.'
> ~~'Did you make any progress?' – 'Yes, little.'~~

> 'Have you had any sleep?' – 'Very little.'
> ~~'Have you had any sleep?' – 'Very a little.'~~

Little and *a little* do not have the same meaning. You use *a little* in a positive way to show that, although you are talking about a small amount or quantity of something, at least there is something. You use *little* in a more negative way, to emphasize that there is only a small amount or quantity of something.

Compare the following:

> *She had brought some food, and we all ate **a little**.*
> *There was some food left over but very **little**.*

Note that both *little* and *a little* are fairly formal when used like this. In informal speech or writing it is more common to say *a bit* or *not much*:

> *She had brought some food, and we all ate **a bit**.*
> *There was food available but **not much**.*

Few *or* a few?

> *I invited some friends and a few came.*
> ~~*I invited some friends and few came.*~~

> *Sweets? – Oh, give me a few!*
> ~~*Sweets? – Oh, give me few!*~~

Few and *a few* do not have the same meaning. You use *a few* to show that you are talking about a small number of people or things.

Few without *a* is much less common. It is used to emphasize that there are only a small number of people or things. Compare the following:

> *There are lots of tourists and **a few** visit this area.*
> *There are lots of tourists but **few** visit this area.*

The first sentence is more positive, saying that although not many tourists visit the area, some do. The second sentence is more negative, emphasizing the fact that not many tourists visit the area.

Note that in conversation and in less formal writing, it is very unusual to use *few* on its own. It is much more common to say *not many*:

> *'Do you have any friends here?'* – '**Not many**.'
> *I like art galleries, but there aren't many here.*

Each/both *or* neither?

> *Neither of them wants it.*
> ~~Each of them doesn't want it.~~

> *Neither was suitable for us.*
> ~~Both weren't suitable for us.~~

Do not use *each* or *both* as the subject of a negative sentence. Use *neither* instead. Remember to use a singular verb after *neither*.

The same as

> *I chose the same as Alex.*
> ~~I chose the same like Alex.~~

> *Your shoes are the same as mine.*
> ~~Your shoes are the same like mine.~~

To say that two things are the same, always say *the same as*.

Enough *or* not enough?

> *Not enough was done to help.*
> ~~Enough was not done to help.~~

> *We didn't provide enough.*
> ~~Enough was not provided.~~

Do not use *enough* as the subject of a negative sentence. Either use *not enough*, or make a sentence in which *enough* is the object of the negative sentence.

Position of pronouns

Both *and* all

We should all go to the cinema.
We all should go to the cinema.

They both live in London.
They live both in London.

You should put *all* or *both* in front of the main verb, not after it or before the auxiliary.

Prepositions

About

> The poem is basically about love.
> ~~The poem is basically on love.~~

> So what's the novel about?
> ~~So what's the novel on?~~

Use *about* to say what subject a book, film, poem, etc. deals with. Do not use *on* for this.

About/around/round

> He owns around/about 200 acres.
> ~~He owns round 200 acres.~~

> She was wearing a scarf around/round her head.
> ~~She was wearing a scarf about her head.~~

Round, *around*, and *about* can often be used with the same meaning. However, to mean 'approximately' use *around* or *about*, and not *round*:

> She's probably **about** twenty.
> I guess **around** thirty people were there.

To mean 'surrounding something' or 'on all sides of something' use *around* or *round*, and not *about*:

> We all sat **round** a table.
> She had a red band **around** her wrist.

Across

> We made our way across the forest.
> ~~We made our way along the forest.~~

> I walked across the dance floor.
> ~~I walked along the dance floor.~~

Use *across* (or *through*) to describe movement from one side of an area to another. Do not use *along*.

Among/amongst

> I wandered among the beautiful trees.
>
> ~~I wandered between the beautiful trees.~~

> The bird was hidden amongst all the leaves.
> ~~The bird was hidden between all the leaves.~~

Do not say that something or someone is or does something *between* many things. For many things, you need to use the preposition *among/amongst*.

As

He works as a waiter in the local restaurant.

~~He works like a waiter in the local restaurant.~~

He is a teacher, like his father.

~~He is a teacher, as his father.~~

Remember that you work *as* a teacher/nurse/plumber, etc. You do not work *like* a teacher/nurse/plumber, etc.

Do not use the preposition *as* to mean 'similar to' or 'in the same way as'. Use *like* for this.

Before

The turning is about a hundred metres before the church.

~~The turning is about a hundred metres in front of the church.~~

Their road is just before the school.

~~Their road is just in front of the school.~~

If you are giving someone directions and you say that one place is a particular distance *before* another place, you mean that they will come to the first place first. Do not use *in front of* with this meaning.

Behind

I parked my motorcycle behind some bushes.

~~I parked my motorcycle behind of some bushes.~~

I hid behind a tree.

~~I hid behind of a tree.~~

Do not say behind *of* something.

Besides

What languages does he speak besides English and Spanish?

~~What languages does he speak except English and Spanish?~~

Did you see anyone else besides Sam?

~~Did you see anyone else except Sam?~~

To mean 'as well as the thing or person mentioned', use *besides*. Do not use *except* for this, which means 'not including something'.

Between

I sat between Greg and Sally.

~~I sat among Greg and Sally.~~

I couldn't see much difference between the three shades.

~~I couldn't see much difference among the three shades.~~

Do not say that you are *among* two people or things. Say that you are *between* them:

She was standing **between** the two men.

Use *between* and not *among* when you are talking about differences. Likewise, use *between* and not *among* to talk about choosing one person or thing from others:

What are the differences **between** the various courses?
It's so difficult to choose **between** the three candidates.

By

Who is the play by?
~~Who is the play from?~~

We'll be finished by three.
~~We'll be finished until three.~~

Use *by* and not *from* to say who wrote a book, play, or piece of music.

If something happens before or at a particular time, you say it happens *by* that time. Do not use *until* for this.

Despite

We had a nice time despite the weather.

~~We had a nice time despite of the weather.~~

Despite the difference in ages, they were close friends.

~~Despite of the difference in ages, they were close friends.~~

Do not say *despite of*.

Also, remember that *despite* is a preposition and cannot be used as a conjunction. You cannot say, for example, ~~Despite we objected, they took our phones away~~. For this, say, *Although we objected, they took our phones away*.

Except

There was no one there except me.
~~There was no one there except I.~~

I didn't know anyone at the party except her.
~~I didn't know anyone at the party except she.~~

Do not use *except* in front of subject pronouns. Use it in front of object pronouns (such as *me*, *him*, or *her*) or reflexive pronouns (such as *himself* or *herself*).

For

I went to Madrid for two weeks.
~~I went to Madrid during two weeks.~~

We've been married for seven years.
~~We've been married since seven years.~~

Use *for*, and not *during* or *since*, when you are stating a period of time (*the weekend*, *three weeks*, *two years*, etc.) in which something happens or is true.

From

He was the headmaster here from 1998 to 2007.
~~He was the headmaster here since 1998 to 2007.~~

The noise continued from nine in the morning till ten o'clock at night.
~~The noise continued since nine in the morning till ten o'clock at night.~~

To say when something began and finished, use *from* and *to/till/until*. Do not use *since* and *to/till/until*.

In

Come in here.
~~Come into here.~~

Put your bags in there.
~~Put your bags into there.~~

Before *here* and *there*, use *in* and not *into*.

In front of

We were waiting in front of the museum.
~~We were waiting in the front of the museum.~~

They gathered in front of the building.
~~They gathered in the front of the building.~~

Do not use *the* before *front* in the prepositional phrase *in front of*.

Inside

I'll meet you inside the café.
~~I'll meet you inside of the café.~~

I wonder what's inside the box.
~~I wonder what's inside of the box.~~

Do not say that someone or something is *inside of* something.

In spite of

It was surprisingly calm in spite of all
the traffic.
~~It was surprisingly calm inspite of all
the traffic.~~

We had a good morning in spite of
the rain.
~~We had a good morning inspite of
the rain.~~

Remember that *in spite of* is three words and not two words.

Remember also that *in spite of* is a compound preposition and cannot be
used as a conjunction. You cannot say, for example, ~~In spite of we objected,
they took our phones away~~. For this, say, *Although we objected, they took our
phones away*.

Near

I was near Coventry when the car broke
down.
~~I was by Coventry when the car broke
down.~~

Mandela was born near Elliotdale.

~~Mandela was born by Elliotdale.~~

Use *near* and not *by* with the names of towns or cities to mean 'close to'.

Remember not to use *close* on its own before a noun. For example, do not
say ~~He lives somewhere close London~~. Use *near* or *close to*:

He lives **near/close to** London.

Of

That's my friend's car.

~~That's the car of my friend.~~

We listened to the President's
speech.
~~We listened to the speech of the
President.~~

You do not usually say 'the something *of* someone' to indicate possessiveness
when the noun phrase you are using is short. Instead, you use -'s after the
noun.

On

I was born on March 11th.
~~I was born in March 11th.~~

On Tuesday, I went shopping.
~~In Tuesday, I went shopping.~~

Do not say that something happens *in* a particular day or date. Say that it happens *on* that day or date.

Onto

They lifted the patient onto the bed.
~~They lifted the patient on the bed.~~

I helped him onto his horse.
~~I helped him on his horse.~~

After many verbs you can use *on* or *onto* with the same meaning. However, after *lift* and verbs which mean 'to lift', you can only use *onto*.

Outside

Jo was standing just outside the school.
~~Jo was standing just outside of the school.~~

I parked outside the hotel.
~~I parked outside of the hotel.~~

Do not say that someone or something is *outside of* something.

Over

Rebecca has over thirty pairs of shoes.
~~Rebecca has above thirty pairs of shoes.~~

We had over eighty applicants.
~~We had above eighty applicants.~~

Use *over* and not *above* in front of a number when you are talking about a quantity or number of things or people.

Round

See about/around/round.

Since

We've lived here since 2005.

~~We've lived here from 2005.~~

I've been doing art classes since February.
~~I've been doing art classes from February.~~

Use *since* and not *from* to say that something began to happen at a particular time in the past and is still happening now.

Note that in sentences like these, you must use a present perfect form before *since*:

> I **haven't eaten** meat **since** I was twelve.
> I**'ve been** wearing glasses **since** I was three.

Through

> We cycled through the forest.
> ~~We cycled along the forest.~~

> I walked through the park.
> ~~I walked along the park.~~

Use *through* (or *across*) to describe movement from one side of an area to another. Do not use *along*.

To

> I go there most days after work.
> ~~I go to there most days after work.~~

> I'm going home in a moment.
> ~~I'm going to home in a moment.~~

Do not use *to* in front of *here* or *there*. Also, do not use *to* in front of *home*.

Do not confuse *to* with *too* and *two*, all of which are pronounced the same.

Towards/toward

> The boat was drifting towards the shore.
> ~~The boat was drifting to the shore.~~

> At the moment, we're heading towards the south of the city.
> ~~At the moment, we're heading to the south of the city.~~

Use *toward(s)* and not *to* in order to show the general direction in which someone or something is moving.

With

> Polish with a soft cloth.
>
> ~~Polish by a soft cloth.~~

> He wiped the sweat off his brow with the back of his hand.
> ~~He wiped the sweat off his brow by the back of his hand.~~

If you explain how something is done by saying which tool or object is used, the usual preposition to use is *with*.

Sentences

Questions

Word order

Where do you live?
~~*Where you do live?*~~

Are you tired?
~~*You are tired?*~~

In questions, you usually put the subject after the first verb. This is the other way round from a statement.

Compare the following:

John *can swim.*
Can **John** *swim?*
There are **five books**.
How many books *are there?*

Questions with auxiliary verbs

Has he been working?
~~*He has been working?*~~

Are you staying here?
~~*You are staying here?*~~

In yes/no questions, if there is an auxiliary verb such as *have* or *be*, the auxiliary verb comes first, followed by the subject and then the main verb.

Using *do*

Do you like it?
~~*You like it?*~~

Did he go to the meeting?
~~*He went to the meeting?*~~

In questions using the present simple, you must use *do* or *does*:

Do *you have a pen?*
Why **does** *he want to see me?*

In questions using the past simple, you must use *did*:

Did *you have a good time?*
When **did** *she meet Max?*

Who, what, etc. as subject

What needs to be done?
What does need to be done?

Who made that noise?
Who did make that noise?

When the *wh-* word is the subject of the sentence, you do not use *do* and the word order is the same as for a statement.

Compare the following:

What did **you** say? ('you' is the subject, 'what' is the object)
What came next? ('what' is the subject)

Negative questions with why?

Why isn't the door locked?
Why the door isn't locked?

Why hasn't Mary called?
Why Mary hasn't called?

Remember to put the subject after the verb in negative questions with *why*.

What is ... like?

What is your house like?
How is your house like?

What were her friends like?
How were her friends like?

If you want to ask someone to describe something, use *What is/are/was/were ... like?* Do not use *how*.

What is ... for?

What is that tool for?
What for is that tool?

What are the red parts for?
What for are the red parts?

To ask about the purpose of something, you should use *What is/are/was/were ... for?* Remember to put *for* at the end of the question.

Indirect questions

Can you tell me where the station is?
~~Can you tell me where is the station?~~

Do you know what time it is?
~~Do you know what is the time?~~

When you ask someone for information, it is polite to use expressions such as *Could you tell me ...?* or *Do you know ...?*. The second part of the question has the same word order as a statement. Do not change the order in the same way as an ordinary question.

Questions in reported speech

She asked me what I was doing.
~~She asked me what was I doing.~~

He asked her why she was crying.
~~He asked her why was she crying.~~

When you use reported speech to tell someone about a question that someone else asked, you use the same word order as for a statement.

Question tags

Isn't she?, won't you?, have you?, etc.

She is very clever, isn't she?
~~*She is very clever, isn't it?*~~

You've been to Spain, haven't you?
~~*You've been to Spain, isn't it?*~~

A question tag is a short phrase that you add to the end of a statement to turn it into a yes/no question. You usually do this when you expect the other person to agree with the statement.

You form a question tag by using the same auxiliary verb, modal verb or form of *be* as in the statement, followed by a personal pronoun. The pronoun refers to the subject of the statement.

Look at the following:

*The weather's nice, **isn't it?***
*We were angry, **weren't we?***
*He's been away, **hasn't he?***

Note that when a statement begins with *I'm* or *I am*, the question tag is *aren't I?*:

*I'm late, **aren't I?***

Remember that the negative forms of modals are often irregular:

*They'll notice that, **won't they?***
*We can go later, **can't we?***

Don't you?, didn't he?, etc.

You like her, don't you?
~~*You like her, isn't it?*~~

You talked to Dave, didn't you?
~~*You talked to Dave, isn't it?*~~

If the statement does not contain an auxiliary verb, a modal verb or *be*, you use the verb *do* in the question tag.

Positive statement, negative tag

> You've got a brother, haven't you?   He doesn't like football, does he?
> ~~You've got a brother, have you?~~   ~~He doesn't like football, doesn't he?~~

You add a negative tag to a positive statement, and a positive tag to a negative statement.

Note, however, that people sometimes add a positive tag to a positive statement, for instance to check that they have understood something correctly, or to show that they are surprised:

> You've been here before, **have you?**
> Oh, you want us to sing, **do you?**

Answers

I hope/think, etc. so

'Is Kate coming?' – 'I expect so.'
~~'Is Kate coming?' – 'I expect it.'~~

'Is Ben married?' – 'I think so.'
~~'Is Ben married?' – 'I think yes.'~~

You use *so* after a reporting verb such as *think*, *expect*, *hope*, and *suppose* to reply positively to something that someone has just said. Do not use *it* or *yes* instead.

However, note that you should not use *so* after *doubt*. Use *it* instead:

'Do your family know you're here?' – 'I doubt **it**.'

I hope/think, etc. not

'Do you think it will rain?' – 'I hope not.'
~~'Do you think it will rain?' – 'I hope no.'~~

'Do you smoke?' – 'Certainly not!'
~~'Do you smoke?' – 'Certainly no!'~~

You use *not* after *hope* and words such as *probably* or *certainly* to reply negatively to something that someone has just said.

You can also use *not* after other reporting verbs such as *think* or *expect*, but this use is rather formal.

Negatives

No, never, not, etc.

None of the children were ready.
~~None of the children weren't ready.~~

Nothing was happening.
~~Nothing wasn't happening.~~

Here is a list of negative words:

neither	none	nothing
never	no one/no-one	nowhere
no	nor	
nobody	not	

If you use one of these words, do not make the verb negative as well.

Not anything/anywhere/anyone

I didn't see anyone.
~~I didn't see someone.~~

I can't find him anywhere.
~~I can't find him nowhere.~~

If you start a sentence with a negative verb, you should not use a negative word such as *nothing* or *nobody* in the second part of the sentence. You should not use *someone*, *something*, or *somewhere* either.

Instead, use *either*, *ever*, *anybody*, *anyone*, *any*, *anything*, or *anywhere*.

Do/does/did not

I don't like cheese.
~~I not like cheese.~~

He didn't hear the news.
~~He not heard the news.~~

If there is no auxiliary or modal verb or the verb *be*, you put *do*, *does*, or *did* after the subject, followed by *not* or *-n't*, followed by the base form of the main verb.

Conjunctions

Although/though

> Although he was late, he stopped to
> chat.
> ~~Although he was late, yet he stopped
> to chat.~~

> Despite his hard work, he failed his
> exam.
> ~~Although his hard work, he failed
> his exam.~~

Although and *though* mean the same but, when used as a conjunction, *though* is slightly less formal.

When a sentence begins with *although* or *though*, do not use *but* or *yet* to introduce the next part of the sentence.

Do not use *although* or *though* in front of a noun or a noun phrase. Use *despite* or *in spite of* instead.

Note that you can put *even* in front of *though*, but not in front of *although*:

> She wore a coat, **even though** it was a hot day.

Because

> Because we'd done a lot of exercise, we
> were all very hungry.
>
> ~~Because we'd done a lot of exercise,
> that is why we were all very hungry.~~

> Because there was no butter,
> I decided not to make a
> sandwich.
> ~~Because there was no butter, that
> is why I decided not to make a
> sandwich.~~

When you use *because* at the beginning of a sentence, do not put a phrase such as *that is why* or *for this reason* at the beginning of the next part of the sentence.

Because *or* because of?

> I was late because there was heavy
> traffic.
> ~~I was late because of there was heavy
> traffic.~~

> I was late because of the heavy
> traffic.
> ~~I was late because the heavy
> traffic.~~

Use *because of* when the next part of the sentence is a noun or a noun phrase. If the next part of the sentence contains a verb, use *because*.

Neither ... nor

> Neither his father nor his mother was there.
>
> ~~His father wasn't there and his mother wasn't there.~~

> She ate neither meat nor fish.
>
> ~~She neither ate meat nor fish.~~

In writing and formal speech, *neither ... nor* is used for linking two words or expressions in order to make a negative statement about both of them. You put *neither* in front of the first word or expression and *nor* in front of the second one.

You always put *neither* immediately in front of the first of the words or expressions that are linked by *nor*. Do not put it any earlier in the sentence.

Remember that *neither ... nor* is rather formal. In speech or informal writing, use sentences such as the following instead:

> His father wasn't there and **neither** was his mother.
> She didn't eat meat **or** fish.

Or

> I don't like coffee or tea.
>
> ~~I don't like coffee and tea.~~

> I didn't see Suzi or Jane.
>
> ~~I didn't see Suzi and Jane.~~

After a negative word, use *or*, not *and* to link two things.

Unless

> I won't go to France unless he pays for my ticket.
>
> ~~I won't go to France unless he will pay for my ticket.~~

> I would go to the party if I didn't have this cold.
>
> ~~I would go to the party unless I had this cold.~~

Do not use a future form after *unless*. When you are talking about the future, you use the present simple after *unless*.

When you are talking about a situation in the past, you use the past simple after **unless**:

> She wouldn't go with him unless **I came** too.

Do not use *unless* to say that something would happen or be true if particular circumstances did not exist. Instead, use if *I didn't*, *if it wasn't*, etc.:

> I'd buy it **if it wasn't** so expensive.
> You'd be less tired **if you didn't** work so hard.

Until

> Stay with me until help comes.
>
> ~~Stay with me until help will come.~~

> I'll wait here until you've had your breakfast.
>
> ~~I'll wait here until you will have had your breakfast.~~

Do not use a future form after *until*. When you are talking about the future, you use the present simple after *until*. When you are talking about something that will be completed by a particular time, you use the present perfect after *until*.

When

> Stop when you feel tired.
>
> ~~Stop when you will feel tired.~~

> I'll come back when you have finished.
>
> ~~I'll come back when you will have finished.~~

Do not use a future form after *when*. When you are talking about the future, you use the present simple after *when*. When you are talking about something that will be completed by a particular time, you use the present perfect after *when*.

Conditionals

Zero conditional

> Water boils when it reaches 100°C.
> ~~Water boils when it will reach 100°C.~~

> My dad gets angry if I am late.
> ~~My dad gets angry, if I am late.~~

The zero conditional is used to talk about things that are always true. You use the present simple in both parts of the sentence. Do not use a comma between the parts of the sentence.

First conditional

> If it rains, we will stay indoors.
>
> ~~If it will rain, we will stay indoors.~~

> He won't succeed unless he is pushed.
> ~~He won't succeed unless he will be pushed.~~

When you are talking about something that might happen in the future, you use the present simple in the conditional clause and *will* or *shall* in the main clause. Do not use *will* or *shall* in both parts of the sentence.

Second conditional

> If they left here, they would never find a job.
> ~~If they would leave here, they would never find a job.~~

> If I won a lot of money, I would buy a big house.
> ~~If I would win a lot of money, I would buy a big house.~~

The second conditional is used for talking about unlikely situations. You use the past simple in the conditional *if-* clause and *would*, *should*, or *might* in the main clause. Do not use *would*, *should*, or *might* in both parts of the sentence.

Note that we often say *were* instead of *was*, especially after *I*:

> If I **were** a guy, I'd probably look like my dad.

Third conditional

If I had seen him, I would have said hello.
~~*If I would have seen him, I would have said hello.*~~

It would have been better if I'd known the truth.
~~*It would have been better if I would have known the truth.*~~

You use the third conditional to talk about something that might have happened in the past but did not happen. Use the past perfect in the conditional *if-* clause and *would have, could have, should have,* or *might have* in the main clause. Do not use *would have, could have, should have,* or *might have* in the main part of the sentence.

Although you may hear people say *would of, could of,* etc. in very informal speech, this is not considered correct, and you should never write it.

If *or* in case?

I will go if he asks me.

~~*I will go in case he asks me.*~~

He qualifies this year if he passes his exams.
~~*He qualifies this year in case he passes his exams.*~~

You do not use *in case* to say that something will happen as a result of something else happening. Use *if* instead.

Relative clauses

Relative pronouns

The man who you met is my brother.

~~The man what you met is my brother.~~

The book that you lent me is very good.

~~The book what you lent me is very good.~~

Relative clauses give extra information about things or people. You need to use a relative pronoun in them. The relative pronouns are *that*, *which*, *who*, and *whom*.

You use *who*, *that*, or *whom* to talk about people:

*We met the people **who** live in the cottage.*
*He was the man **that** bought my house.*
*He was a distant relative **whom** I never met.* (Formal)

You use *which* or *that* to talk about things:

*It's a type of pasta **which** comes from Milan.*
*There are a lot of things **that** are wrong.*

What is not a relative pronoun, and should not be used in a relative clause.

No extra pronoun

The town where I work is near London.

~~The town where I work, it is near London.~~

This is the book which I bought yesterday.

~~This is the book which I bought it yesterday.~~

The relative pronoun in a relative clause acts as the subject or object of the clause. Do not add another pronoun as the subject or object.

Commas in defining clauses

The woman who works in the shop is my sister.

~~The woman, who works in the shop, is my sister.~~

My father, who is in London today, asked me to tell you.

~~My father who is in London today asked me to tell you.~~

Defining relative clauses give information that helps to identify the person or thing you are talking about. Do not put commas around these clauses:

*The table **that you gave me** is broken.*

Non-defining relative clauses give extra information about a person or thing, but do not help to identify them. You must put commas in front of these clauses, and after them if the sentence continues:

*He was waving to the girl**, who was running along the platform**.*
*The book**, which I enjoyed very much,** was by a Polish author.*

Which or that?

I teach at the college, which is just over the road.	*The money, which he spent on cars, came from his aunt.*
~~I teach at the college, that is just over the road.~~	~~The money, that he spent on cars, came from his aunt.~~

When a non-defining clause relates to a thing or a group of things, you use *which*. Do not use *that*.

Who or whom?

My aunt, who lives in a remote area, does not have broadband.	*This is the woman to whom he gave the money.*
~~My aunt, whom lives in a remote area, does not have broadband.~~	~~This is the woman to who he gave the money.~~

You always use *who* as the subject of a defining clause. You can use *who* or *whom* as the object. *Whom* is more formal:

*I was in the same group as Janice, **who/whom** I like a lot.*
*This is the man **who/whom** I met at Jack's.*

However, if there is a preposition before the relative pronoun, you should use *whom*:

*Paul was the son **to whom** he had given the money.*

Whose

> Freeman, whose book is published this
> week, would not comment.
> ~~Freeman, that book is published this~~
> ~~week, would not comment.~~

> This is a story whose purpose is to
> entertain.
> ~~This is a story which purpose is to~~
> ~~entertain.~~

You use a noun phrase containing *whose* at the beginning of a relative clause to show who or what something belongs to or is connected with. Do not use any other relative pronoun for this.

Phrases

In my opinion

In my opinion, this practice is immoral.
~~*According to me, this practice is immoral.*~~

I believe that this is wrong.
~~*According to me, this is wrong.*~~

You can say *according to John/my dad/the manager*, etc., but it is incorrect to say ~~*according to me*~~. Instead of this, use phrases such as *I believe*, *I think*, and *in my opinion*.

Note also that it is incorrect to say *according to someone's opinion*. For example, do not say ~~*According to the bishop's opinion, the public has a right to know*~~. Say instead, *The bishop's opinion is that the public has a right to know*.

Burst into tears

She burst into tears and ran out of the classroom.
~~*She burst in tears and ran out of the classroom.*~~

I told my son and he burst into tears.
~~*I told my son and he burst in tears.*~~

Remember that this phrase is *burst into tears* and not ~~*burst in tears*~~.

Be looking forward to something

I'm really looking forward to seeing you.
~~*I'm really looking forwards to seeing you.*~~

I bet you're looking forward to the holidays!
~~*I bet you're looking forwards to the holidays!*~~

Note that the word in this phrase is *forward* and not ~~*forwards*~~.

Get to know someone

I'd like to get to know her a bit better.
~~*I'd like to know her a bit better.*~~

I've enjoyed getting to know Sam over the last few weeks.
~~*I've enjoyed knowing Sam over the last few weeks.*~~

To express the idea of starting to know someone after spending time with them, use the phrase *get to know* someone. It is incorrect simply to use *know* for this.

I don't mind

> 'Shall we go now or a bit later?' – 'I don't mind.'
>
> ~~'Shall we go now or a bit later?' – 'I don't mind it.'~~

> 'Red wine or white?' – 'I don't mind.'
>
> ~~'Red wine or white?' – 'I don't mind it.'~~

Remember that if you want to reply to someone, saying that you are happy with either of two or more options, the phrase is *I don't mind*. Do not say ~~I don't mind it~~.

There is no point in doing something

> There's no point in calling her now.
>
> ~~There's no point to call her now.~~

> There's no point in getting angry with him!
>
> ~~It's no point in getting angry with him!~~

To say that a particular action would not achieve anything, say *There is no point in doing* something. Do not say ~~It's no point in doing~~ something, or ~~There is no point to do~~ something.

Collocation

Collocation is the way that words go together in a natural way. For example, we say *commit a crime*, *heavy traffic*, and *bitterly disappointed*. Many of these word combinations are difficult or impossible to guess, but your English will not sound correct if you get them wrong. This section of the book covers some collocations which learners often find difficult.

Make *or* do?

I made a big effort.
~~I did a big effort.~~

He is doing his homework.
~~He is making his homework.~~

It is very common to make errors with *make* or *do*. Although they have similar meanings, you must use the right one.

Do not use *do* to talk about creating something. For example, you *make a cake*, *make a piece of furniture*, etc.

Be especially careful with the following:

Make

He finds it difficult to **make friends**.
We **made** *a big* **effort** *to help him*.
You have **made** *a lot of* **mistakes**.
They **made** *some* **changes** *to the course*.
She **made** *lots of* **excuses** *for her poor work*.
I need to **make** *a* **list** *before I go shopping*.
We have **made** *a lot of* **progress**.

Do

Have you **done** *your* **homework** *yet?*
We need to **do** *more* **research** *in this area*.
We have **done** *a lot of* **work** *today*.
I never **do business** *with criminals*.

Other verb + noun collocations

We're having a party for Jamie.
~~We're making a party for Jamie.~~

She committed a terrible crime.
~~She did a terrible crime.~~

Here are some more important verb + noun collocations which often cause mistakes. Use the verbs shown here, and do not use other verbs instead:

get on/off a bus, train, etc. (Not ~~get/go into~~ or ~~get/go out of~~)
have children (Not ~~get~~)
give a demonstration (Not ~~make~~)
have a dream (Not ~~dream a dream~~)

take an exam/a test (Not ~~make~~. Remember also that *pass a test/an exam* means to be successful in it.)
give an example (Not ~~say~~)
have an experience (Not ~~make~~)
conduct/do an experiment (Not ~~make~~)
tell a joke/lies (Not ~~say~~)
get/have permission (Not ~~take~~)

Talking about size, amount, and degree

There was a large amount of food.   *We heard a loud noise.*
~~There was a big amount of food.~~   ~~We heard a big noise.~~

When you talk about the size, amount, or degree of something, some adjectives sound much more natural than others.

You usually talk about a *large* or *small* number, amount, or quantity of something (not *big/high/little* or *low*).

Here are some other common collocations connected with size and amount that often cause mistakes:

*There was a **large/wide/narrow choice** of subjects.* (Not ~~big/small, little~~)
*This issue is of **great importance** to us.* (Not ~~big~~)
*Maria has made **great/a lot of progress** recently.* (Not ~~big~~)
*He's a very **tall man**.* (Not ~~high~~)
*She was in **great pain**.* (Not ~~bad~~)

Which Word?

The words in this section are often used incorrectly. There are several reasons for this:

- Some (eg *glad* and *happy*), have similar meanings, but are used in different grammatical structures.
- Some words which look similar in other languages have different meanings. For example, the English word *library* means a place where you borrow books, but the similar word in several other languages means a shop where you buy books.
- Some (eg *high* and *tall*) have different collocations. Although the meaning is similar, they are used with different words.

Able *or* capable?

Able and *capable* are both used to say that someone can do something. However, they are used with different patterns. Use *able + to-* infinitive, and *capable + of + -ing* verb:

> *We were able to see the horses.*
> *Is he capable of managing a team?*

You can also use *capable of* + noun:

> *She's capable of some really good work.*

Accept *or* agree?

Do not say that you *accept* to do what someone suggests. You say that you *agree* to do it:

> *She agreed to talk to him.*

Actual, current, *or* present?

You do not use *actual* to describe something currently happening, being done, or being used at the present time. Use *current* or *present* instead.

> *I couldn't hear his actual words.*
> *The current situation is very difficult.*
> *We are not in contact at the present time.*

Actually, currently, or at the moment?

You use *actually* to emphasize that something is true, especially if it is surprising:

*I was told that Suzie was bad-tempered, but **actually** she was really nice.*

Do not use *actually* when you want to say that something is happening now. Use *currently* (rather formal) or *at the moment* instead:

*The company **currently** employs 50 staff.*
*I'm learning French **at the moment**.*

Alone, lonely, or on your own?

People who are *alone* have nobody with them. You can also say that someone is *on their own* with the same meaning. If you are *lonely*, you are unhappy because you do not have any friends or anyone to talk to. *Alone* cannot be used in front of a noun:

They left us alone in the room.
I was on my own that day.
She was very lonely without any of her friends.

Amount or number?

Do not use *amount* in front of plural countable nouns. Use *number* instead. Use *amount* in front of uncountable nouns:

We only need a small amount of money.
There were a large number of people there.

Anniversary or birthday?

An *anniversary* is a date when you remember something special that happened on that date in an earlier year. Do not use *anniversary* for the date when you were born. This is your *birthday*:

It's our wedding anniversary today.
It's the fifth anniversary of his death.
When is your birthday?

Announcement *or* advertisement?

An *announcement* is a public statement giving information about something. An *advertisement* is an item in a newspaper, on TV, on the internet, etc. that tries to persuade you to buy something:

The chancellor made an announcement about the crisis earlier today.
He bought the game after seeing an advertisement on TV.

Argument *or* discussion?

Do not use *discussion* to refer to a disagreement. This is usually called an *argument*. A *discussion* is a fairly long conversation about something:

We had an interesting discussion about religion.
We had a terrible argument, and now she won't talk to me.

Ashamed *or* embarrassed?

If you are *ashamed*, you feel sorry about something you did wrong. If you are *embarrassed*, you are worried that people will think you are silly:

They were ashamed to admit they had lied.
I felt really embarrassed about singing in public.

Assist *or* be present?

If you *assist* someone, you help them. *Assist* is a formal word. If you want to say that someone is there when something happens, you say that they *are present*:

We may be able to assist with the fees.
He was present at the birth of his son.

Avoid *or* prevent?

If someone does not allow you to do what you want to do, do not say that they *avoid* you doing it. Say that they *prevent* you *from* doing it:

He tried to avoid breathing in the smoke.
I wanted to prevent him from speaking.

Blame *or* fault?

Do not say that something is someone's *blame*. You say that it is their *fault*, or that they are *to blame for* it:

I knew I was partly to blame for the failure of the project.
It's not our fault if the machine breaks down.

Borrow, lend, *or* use?

If you *borrow* something that belongs to someone else, you use it for a period of time, then return it. If you *lend* something you own to someone else, you allow them to use it for a period of time.

You do not usually talk about *borrowing* or *lending* things that can't move. It is more common to say *use* for this:

Can I borrow your pen?
I'll lend you some money.
Can I use your washing machine?

Bring, take, *or* fetch?

If you *bring* something, you carry or move it to the place where you are. If you *take* something, you carry or move it to another place. If you *fetch* something, you go to the place where it is and return with it:

Could you bring your laptop with you?
She gave me some books to take home.
Could you fetch me a glass of water, please?

Buy *or* pay?

Do not say that you will *pay* someone a drink, meal, etc. Instead, say you will *buy* them a drink, or that you will *pay for* the drink:

Let me buy you a drink.
I'll pay for the taxi.

Carry *or* take?

Carry and *take* are used to say that someone moves a person or thing from one place to another. When you use *carry*, you are showing that the person or thing is quite heavy, and that you have them in your hands or arms:

> *My father carried us on his shoulders.*
> *She gave me the books to **take** home.*

Certain *or* sure?

You can say that you are *certain of* or *sure of* something, meaning that you have no doubts about it.

You can say that it is *certain that* something will happen, but do not say ~~it is sure that~~ something will happen:

> *I'm sure/certain he's right.*
> *It seemed certain that they would succeed.*

Certainly, definitely, *or* surely?

You use *certainly* and *definitely* to emphasize that something is true. However, you use *surely* to express disagreement or surprise:

> *It certainly looks good, doesn't it?*
> *She definitely deserves to win.*
>
> *Surely you haven't lost your glasses again?*
> *Surely he's not as bad as you say.*

Cloth, clothes, *or* clothing?

There is no singular form of *clothes* but you can talk about *a piece of clothing* or *an item of clothing*.

You often use *clothing* to talk about the type of clothes people wear, eg *winter clothing*, *warm clothing*, etc.

Cloth is fabric such as wool or cotton. In this meaning, it is an uncountable noun:

> *I cut up strips of cotton cloth.*

Control or check/inspect?

If someone *controls* someone or something, they have the power to decide what they do or what happens to them. Do not use *control* as a verb to mean *check* or *inspect*:

His family had controlled the company for more than a century.
I had to wait while my luggage was being checked.

Cook or cooker?

Remember that a *cooker* is a piece of equipment, not a person. A person who cooks, especially as a job, is a *cook*:

I turned on the cooker.
Abigail is an excellent cook.

Employ or use?

Although you can say that something is *employed* for a particular purpose, this is very formal. In less formal writing, or in speech, the normal word is *use*:

A number of techniques are employed.
He used a hammer to bang in the nails.

Especially or specially?

You use *especially* to show that what you are saying applies more to one thing or situation than to others. You use *specially* to say that something is done or made for a particular purpose:

He was kind to his staff, especially those who were sick or in trouble.
They'd come down specially to see us.

Eventually or possibly/perhaps?

When something happens after a lot of delays or problems, you can say that it *eventually* happens. Do not use *eventually* when you mean that something might be true. Use *possibly* or *perhaps*:

Eventually, they got to the hospital.
Perhaps he'll call later.

Far/far away/a long way away

You use *far* in questions and negative sentences to mean 'a long distance'. Do not use *far* like this in positive sentences. Instead, say that somewhere is *far away* or *a long way away*:

How far is it to your house?
The office is a long way from the city centre.
He lives quite far away from here.

Note also that you should not use *far* when you are stating a distance. Instead, you should say that a place is a particular distance *from* somewhere, or that it is a particular distance *away*:

The hotel is just fifty metres from the ocean.
The nearest city is 10 miles away.

Female *or* feminine?

Female means 'relating to the sex that can have babies'. *Feminine* means 'typical of women rather than men':

We want to see more female managers.
The bedroom has a light, feminine look.

Fit *or* suit?

If clothes *fit* you, they are the right size for you. If they *suit* you, they make you look attractive:

That dress fits you perfectly.
You look great in that dress – it really suits you.

Friendly *or* sympathetic?

A *friendly* person is kind and pleasant. A *sympathetic* person shows that they are sorry if you have problems:

My new colleagues seem very friendly.
I was ill, but he wasn't at all sympathetic.

Gain or earn?

If you *gain* something, such as an ability or quality, you gradually get more of it. If you *earn* money, you are paid for the work you do:

This gives you a chance to gain some experience.
She earns £200 a week.

Glad or happy?

Glad and *happy* are both used to say that people are pleased about something:

I'm so glad that you passed the exam.
She was happy that his sister was coming.

You can also use *happy* to describe someone who is contented and enjoys life. Do not use *glad* with this meaning, and do not use *glad* in front of a noun:

She always seemed such a happy woman.

Hear or listen to?

If you *hear* something, you become aware of its sound, often without trying to. If you *listen to* something, you deliberately pay attention to it:

Listen carefully to what he says.
Suddenly, I heard a noise.

High or tall?

You use both *high* and *tall* to describe things which are a large distance from bottom to top. However, you use *tall* to describe things that are also much higher than they are wide. You always use *tall* to describe people:

The place is surrounded by high mountains.
There was a tall tree next to the house.
My sister is very tall.

Hope *or* wish?

Do not use *wish* with a *that-* clause to express a wish for the future. For example, do not say ~~I wish you'll have a nice time in Finland~~. Use *hope* for that:

I hope you'll have a nice time in Finland.

Library *or* bookshop?

A *library* is a building where books are kept that people can look at or borrow. Do not use *library* for a place that sells books. This is a *bookshop* in UK English and a *bookstore* in US English:

You can borrow the book from your local library.
The book is available in all good bookshops.

Male *or* masculine?

Male means 'relating to the sex that cannot have babies'. *Masculine* means 'typical of men rather than women':

Male dogs tend to be more aggressive.
He was strong, tall, and very masculine.

Marriage *or* wedding?

Marriage refers to the state of being married, or to the relationship of two people who are married. *Wedding* is used for the ceremony where two people get married:

They had a long and happy marriage.
We were invited to their wedding.

Nervous, anxious, *or* annoyed?

If you are *nervous*, you are worried about something you are going to do or experience. Do not use *nervous* when you are worried about something that might happen to someone else. Use *anxious* for that:

My daughter is nervous about starting school.
It's time to go home – your mother will be anxious.

Do not use *nervous* to mean 'angry and impatient' – use *annoyed* or *irritated* for that:

I was annoyed by his questions.

Parking *or* car park?

Do not use the word *parking* to refer to a place where cars are parked. Instead, say *car park* in UK English and *parking lot* in US English. *Parking* is only used to refer to the action of parking your car or the state of being parked:

We parked in the car park next to the theatre.
Parking in the city centre is very difficult.

People *or* persons?

The usual plural of *person* is *people*. However, *persons* is sometimes used in very formal English:

How many people have you invited?
No unauthorized persons may enter the building.

Prove *or* test?

If you *prove* that something is correct, you provide evidence showing that it is definitely true or correct. When you use a practical method to try to find out how good or bad someone or something is, do not say that you *prove* them. Use *test* for this:

He was able to prove that he was an American.
A number of new techniques were tested.

Remember *or* remind?

If you mention to someone that they had intended to do something, do not say that you *remember* them to do it. Use *remind* for this:

He remembered to turn the gas off.
I reminded her to call her mother.

Rob *or* steal?

You use *rob* in reference to a person or a place, and *steal* in reference to the thing that is stolen:

> *He was robbed on his way home.*
> *They robbed a bank.*
> *She stole a bike.*

See, look at, *or* watch?

When you *see* something, you are aware of it through your eyes, often without trying to be. When you *look at* something, you direct your eyes towards it. When you *watch* something, you pay attention to it for a period of time, using your eyes, because you are interested in what it is doing, or what may happen:

> *I waved, but nobody saw me.*
> *He looked at the food on his plate.*
> *We watched the sunset.*

Remember that we say *watch TV/watch the television*. Do not use *see* or *look at* for this.

Shadow *or* shade?

A *shadow* is a dark shape made on a surface when something stands between a light and the surface. *Shade* is an area that is dark and cool because the sun cannot reach it:

> *My shadow was long in the evening sun.*
> *We sat in the shade.*

Souvenir *or* memory?

A *souvenir* is an object you buy or keep to remind you of a special time or place. Do not use *souvenir* to talk about something that you remember. Use *memory* for this:

> *He kept the spoon as a souvenir of his journey.*
> *I have some very happy memories of that time.*

Spend *or* pass?

If someone does something from the beginning to the end of a period of time, you say that they *spend* the period of time doing it. Do not use *pass* for this. Use *pass* to talk about doing something to occupy yourself while you are waiting for something:

We spent the morning talking about art.
To pass the time they played games.

Strange *or* unusual?

You use *strange* to say that something is unfamiliar or unexpected in a way that makes you puzzled, uneasy, or afraid. If you just want to say that something is not common, you use *unusual*, not *strange*:

He has some very strange ideas about education.
He had an unusual name.

Support *or* stand/put up with, etc.?

Do not use *support* to say that someone accepts pain or an unpleasant situation, or that someone allows something they do not approve of. Use *stand*, *put up with*, *bear*, or *tolerate* (formal) instead:

I can't bear his constant complaining.
I've put up with his bad behaviour for too long.

Understand *or* realize?

Do not use *understand* to say that someone becomes aware of something. Use *realize* for this:

Her accent was hard to understand.
I didn't realize how late it was.

Win, defeat, *or* beat?

Do not use *win* in front of the name of an enemy or an opponent. For games or contests, use *beat* or (slightly more formal) *defeat*, and for wars or battles, use *defeat*:

We won the game easily.
She beat him at chess.
They were defeated in the battle of Waterloo.

Confusable Words

Words that sound the same

The words in this section are **homophones** (words that sound the same, but are spelled differently). It is easy to confuse them.

affect *Affect* is a verb: *How will this new law affect me?*	**effect** *Effect* is a noun: *What will the effect of the new law be?*
already *Already* is an adverb. If something has *already* happened, it has happened before the present time: *I've already called an ambulance.*	**all ready** In the phrase *all ready*, *all* is a quantifier meaning the whole of a group or a thing, and *ready* is an adjective: *Are you all ready to go?*
alter *Alter* is a verb, meaning 'to change': *Nothing in the house had altered since 1960.*	**altar** An *altar* is the holy table in a church: *The priest stood in front of the altar.*
aural *Aural* means 'connected with your ears and your sense of hearing': *We had an aural test in music.*	**oral** *Oral* means 'relating to your mouth'. It also describes things that involve speaking rather than listening: *We do a lot of oral work in Spanish.*
bare *Bare* is an adjective meaning 'not covered' or 'not wearing any clothes': *We ran along the beach with bare feet.*	**bear** A *bear* is a wild animal: *There are bears in the woods.* *Bear* is also a verb: *I can't bear spiders.*
base The *base* of something is its lowest edge or part: *I had a pain in the base of my spine.*	**bass** A *bass* is a male singer who can sing very low notes. *Bass* instruments play low notes: *She plays bass guitar.*
board A *board* is a flat piece of wood: *They nailed a board over the window.*	**bored** If you are *bored*, you are not interested by something: *I was so bored at school today.*

break
If you *break* something or if it *breaks*, it divides into two or more pieces, often as the result of an accident:
He fell through the window, breaking the glass.

brake
A *brake* is a device on a vehicle that makes it slow down or stop. *Brake* is also a verb:
He took his foot off the brake.
The driver braked suddenly.

coarse
Coarse is an adjective meaning 'having a rough texture' or 'talking and behaving in a rude way':
The sand was very coarse.
His manners are coarse.

course
Course is a noun with several meanings, including 'a series of lessons' and 'a route or path':
The plane changed course.
I did a course in art history.

compliment
A *compliment* is a nice thing that someone says about someone or something. *Compliment* can also be used as a verb:
They paid him a lot of compliments.
She complimented me on my roses.

complement
If people or things *complement* each other, they have different qualities that go well together:
The dry wine complements this rich dish perfectly.

counsellor
A *counsellor* gives people advice, often on personal matters, such as relationships and jobs:
They went to see a marriage counsellor.

councillor
A *councillor* is an official in a local council:
She was elected as a councillor last year.

current
A *current* is the flowing movement of water, for example in a river:
There is a strong current here.
Current is also an adjective which describes things that are happening or existing now:
Our current methods of production are too expensive.

currant
A *currant* is a small, dried grape:
I put currants in the cakes.

dependent
Dependent is an adjective. If you are *dependent on* someone or something, you rely on them:
Their economy is very dependent on oil.

dependant
Dependant is a noun. Your *dependants* are the people you are financially responsible for:
He has a large income and no dependants.

discreet
If you are *discreet*, you are careful to avoid attracting attention or revealing private information:
I made a few discreet inquiries about her.

discrete
If things are *discrete*, they are not joined or connected in any way:
I met him on three discrete occasions.

draft
A *draft* of a piece of writing is a first, rough version of it:
He showed me the first draft of his story.

draught
A *draught* is a current of air:
There's a draught coming in through that window.

Note that in US English, this is spelled *draft*.

draw
Draw is a verb meaning 'to make a picture with a pencil':
Shall we draw a picture?

drawer
A *drawer* is part of a desk, cupboard, etc.:
I put the papers away in a drawer.

ensure
In UK English, *ensure* means 'to make certain that something happens'. In US English, the word is usually spelled *insure*:
Please ensure your phones are switched off.

insure
If you *insure* something, you pay money to a company so that if it is lost, stolen, or damaged, the company will pay you a sum of money:
Insure your baggage before you leave home.

hole
A *hole* is an opening or a hollow space in something:
There's a hole in my shoe.

whole
Whole is a quantifier meaning 'all of something':
He ate the whole loaf.

its
Its means 'belonging to it':
The dog wagged its tail.

it's
It's means 'it is':
It's going to be difficult to fit in all this work.

led
Led is the past participle of the verb 'lead':
He led me into a small room.

lead
Lead is a noun, meaning 'a soft, grey metal':
The roof is covered with lead.

Lead is also a verb, but it has a different pronunciation.

licence *Licence* is a noun: *I showed him my driving licence.*	**license** *License* is a verb: *We are not licensed to serve alcohol.* Note that in US English, *licence* is used for the verb and the noun.
practice *Practice* is a noun: *I did my piano practice.*	**practise** *Practise* is a verb: *I practised the piano.* Note that in US English, *practice* is used for the verb and the noun.
principle *Principle* is a noun meaning 'a belief about what is right or wrong' or 'a basic rule': *Eating meat is against my principles.* *We learned the basic principles of yoga.*	**principal** *Principal* is an adjective meaning 'most important': *Bad weather was the principal reason for the failure of the expedition.* *Principal* can also be a noun meaning 'the person in charge of a school or college': *She was sent to the principal's office.*
role Your *role* is your position and what you do in a situation or society: *His role was to check the tickets.* A *role* is also one of the characters that an actor plays: *She played the role of Ophelia.*	**roll** A *roll* is a small, round loaf of bread: *I had a cheese roll for lunch.* A *roll* of something, such as cloth or paper, is a long piece of it wrapped many times around itself or around a tube: *A bought a roll of wallpaper.*
site A *site* is an area that is used for a particular purpose or where something happens: *He works on a building site.* *This is the site of the explosion.*	**sight** *Sight* is the ability to see, and a sight is something you can see: *She lost her sight in an accident.* *I faint at the sight of blood.*
stationery *Stationery* is a noun meaning 'paper, envelopes, and writing equipment': *Envelopes are kept in the stationery cupboard.*	**stationary** *Stationary* is an adjective meaning 'not moving': *I drove into a stationary vehicle.*

story A *story* is something you read in a book: *I bought a book of fairy stories.*	**storey** A *storey* is a level of a building: *My office is in a six storey building.*
whether *Whether* is a conjunction used to talk about a choice or doubt between two or more alternatives: *I can't decide whether to have soup or salad.*	**weather** *Weather* is a noun we use to talk about rain, snow, sun, etc.: *The weather was great in Portugal.*
whose *Whose* is a pronoun and a determiner used to ask questions about who something belongs to, or to talk about things connected to a particular person: *Whose shoes are these?* *He helped a woman whose face was covered with blood.*	**who's** *Who's* means 'who is': *Who's going to do the washing up?*
witch *Witch* is a noun, meaning 'an evil magic woman': *We painted a witch on a broomstick.*	**which** *Which* is a pronoun and a determiner used to ask questions when there are two or more possible alternatives, or to talk about things connected to a particular person: *Which is your cabin?* *I took the coat which looked warmest.*
your *Your* is a pronoun showing that something belongs to you or relates to you: *Where is your car?*	**you're** *You're* means 'you are': *You're late again.*

These groups of three words are among the most commonly misused words in English. They are all extremely frequent, so it is important that you are confident about using them correctly.

they're	*They're* means 'they are': *They're going to come on the train,* *I'll be angry if they're late again.*
their	*Their* is the possessive pronoun from 'they': *They forgot to bring their coats.* *Their faces were white and tear-stained.*
there	*There* is a pronoun and adverb used to show position or direction, to show that something exists, and at the beginning of many sentences and phrases: *There's your jacket.* *Can you see the lion over there?* *The old buildings are still there today.* *There must be another way of doing this.* *There are three churches in our town.*
too	*Too* is used before adjectives to mean 'more than is good': *It's too hot in here.* It also means 'as well': *I want some too.*
to	*To* is a preposition that is used in many ways, but the main ones are showing direction, showing who receives something, and forming the infinitive: *We went to the zoo.* *I gave it to John.* *I need to buy a new coat.*
two	*Two* is the number 2: *I have two brothers.*
we're	*We're* means 'we are': *We're having a party.* *I'll phone you when we're there.*
were	*Were* is the past tense of *be* when the subject is plural: *We were very happy.* *They were going to tell you.*
where	*Where* is used to talk about the location of things or to ask questions about the location of things: *Where do you live?* *I left the keys where Julie would be sure to find them.*

Other words that are often confused

These words do not sound the same, but they are spelled in quite a similar way, and often cause confusion:

accept *Accept* is a verb and means 'agree to have': *I cannot accept money from you.*	**except** *Except* is a preposition and a conjunction meaning 'not including': *Everyone was invited except Flora.*
advice *Advice* is a noun: *Can you give me some advice about growing roses?*	**advise** *Advise* is a verb: *I advised him to wait a bit longer.*
alternate *Alternate* things happen regularly, one after the other. If something happens on *alternate* days, weeks, etc., it happens on one day/week, not on the next, then happens again the day/week after that: *She spends alternate weeks with her father.*	**alternative** You use *alternative* to describe something that can be used, had, or done instead of something else: *I suggested an alternative approach.*
arise When an opportunity, problem, or situation *arises*, it begins to exist: *A serious problem has arisen.*	**rise** When something or someone *rises*, they move upward: *He rose to greet her.* *Rise* also means to increase: *Prices have risen.*
bath *Bath* is a noun: *I had a bath.* You can say that you *bath* someone, especially a baby: *She showed us how to bath the baby.*	**bathe** *Bathe* is a verb. In US English, you can say that people *bathe*: *He went home to bathe.* In UK English, you say *have a bath* instead. In US and UK English, you can say that you *bathe* a wound, meaning to clean it with water. *Bathe* is not used in modern English to mean *go swimming*.

beside
Beside means 'next to':
Put the chair beside the window.

besides
Besides means 'as well' or 'in addition to':
I don't need any help. Besides, I've nearly finished.
He designed houses, office blocks, and much else besides.

breath
Breath is a noun:
She took a deep breath.

breathe
Breathe is a verb:
Try to breathe through your nose.

close (verb)
If you *close* something, you shut it:
Please close the door.

close (adjective)
Something *close* is not far away:
We live close to the city centre.

continual
Continual is used to mean that something happens without interruption, and also that something happens repeatedly:
I'm fed up with this continual noise.
There have been continual demands for action.

continuous
Continuous is only used for things that happen without interruption and do not stop at all:
He has a continuous buzzing sound in his ear.

dead
Dead is an adjective:
The woman was clearly dead.

died
Died is the past tense and past participle of the verb *die*:
She died last week.

definite
If something is *definite*, it is firm and clear and not likely to be changed:
Do we have a definite date for the meeting?

definitive
Something that is *definitive* provides a firm, unquestionable conclusion:
No one has come up with a definitive answer.

dessert
A *dessert* is the sweet dish you eat at the end of a meal:
Shall we have a dessert?

desert
A *desert* is a large, dry, sandy area:
We travelled through the Sahara Desert.

elder
Elder is used when you are saying which of two people was born first. It is not used with *than*:
I live with my elder sister.
He is the elder of the two.

older
Older simply means 'more old', and can be used of people or things, and can be followed by *than*:
My car is older than yours.

infer
If you *infer* something, you draw a conclusion from what you have seen, heard, or read:
From his resignation letter, I inferred that he had been forced to leave.

imply
If you *imply* something, you say it in an indirect way:
She implied that he owed her money.

lay
Lay is a transitive verb meaning 'to put something somewhere carefully', and must have an object:
Mothers often lay babies on their backs to sleep.

It is not correct to say *I'm going to lay down* – you should use *lie* for this.

Lay is also the past tense of *lie*:
We lay on the floor.

lie
Lie is an intransitive verb meaning 'to be in a horizontal position':
I want to lie down.

loose
Loose is an adjective meaning 'not firmly fixed':
The bolts had worked loose.

lose
Lose is a verb meaning 'to not have something any more' or 'to be defeated':
I'm always losing my keys.
I think we're going to lose the match.

personal
Personal is an adjective meaning 'private' or 'relating to a particular person':
He asked me some very personal questions.
She has her own personal helicopter.

personnel
Personnel is a noun meaning 'the people who work in an organization':
All military personnel must report to base.

price
The *price* of something is the amount of money that you must pay to buy it:
The price of a cup of coffee is almost five dollars.

prize
A *prize* is something given to someone for winning a competition:
He won a prize in a painting competition.

quite
Quite is an adverb and used to mean 'very' in a less emphatic way:
It was quite expensive.

quiet
Quiet is an adjective and describes things or people that do not make much noise:
She had a very quiet voice.

raise	**rise**
Raise is a transitive verb: *He raised his cup to his lips.* *Prices have been raised.*	*Rise* is an intransitive verb: *Columns of smoke rose into the sky.* *Prices rose by more than 10%.*
sensible A *sensible* person makes good decisions and judgments based on reason rather than emotion: *She was a sensible girl and did not panic.*	**sensitive** A *sensitive* person is easily upset or offended: *He is quite sensitive about his weight.* You also use *sensitive* to mean that someone shows awareness and understanding of other people's feelings: *The police were very sensitive in the way they dealt with the situation.*
suppose *Suppose* is a verb. If you *suppose* that something is true, you think it is probably true: *I suppose it was difficult.*	**supposed to** If something is *supposed to* be done, it should be done because of a rule, instruction, etc.: *I'm not supposed to talk to you about this.* If something is *supposed to* be true, most people think it is true: *It's supposed to be a good movie.*

Topics

Numbers

Six hundred/eight thousand, etc.

We drove over six hundred miles.

~~We drove over six hundreds miles.~~

Over seven thousand people attended.

~~Over seven thousands people attended.~~

Hundred, thousand, million, and *billion* remain singular even when the number before them is greater than one.

Six hundred people/eight thousand dollars, etc.

Thirty children came to the party.

~~Thirty of children came to the party.~~

Over three million people are now unemployed.

~~Over three million of people are now unemployed.~~

Do not use *of* after the words *hundred, thousand, million,* and *billion* when referring to an exact number.

Two hundred and three

two thousand, eight hundred, and forty
~~two thousand, eight hundred, forty~~

six hundred and twenty-three
~~six hundred, twenty-three~~

Numbers over 100 are generally written in figures. However, in UK English, if you want to say them or to write them in words, you put *and* in front of the number expressed by the last two figures:

Four hundred and eighteen (418) *men were killed on that day.*

Note that in US English, leaving out *and* here is acceptable.

The only three … /the following four …

Consider the following four questions.

~~Consider the four following questions.~~

They were the only three people who replied.

~~They were the three only people who replied.~~

When you put a number and an adjective in front of a noun (for example, *three small children*) you usually put the number in front of the adjective. However, in the case of the adjectives *only* and *following*, you put the number after the adjective.

Ten years/three hundred pounds, etc. is …

Three thousand dollars is a lot of money.

~~Three thousand dollars are a lot of money.~~

110 kilos is too much!

~~110 kilos are too much!~~

When you use any number except one in front of a noun, you use a plural noun and a plural verb. However, when you are talking about an amount of money, a period of time, or a distance, speed, or weight, you usually use a singular verb.

The third/a fourth, etc. (of something)

There are two problems. The first relates to money, the second to time.

~~There are two problems. First relates to money and second to time.~~

Ben was the second of three sons.

~~Ben was second of three sons.~~

When you use an ordinal number (*first, second, third,* etc.) as a pronoun, you must use a determiner before it.

Time

a.m./p.m.

The flight leaves at 3 p.m.

Our office hours are 9 a.m. to 5 p.m.

~~*The flight leaves at 3 o'clock p.m.*~~

~~*Our office hours are 9 o'clock a.m. to 5 o'clock p.m.*~~

Do not use *a.m.* or *p.m.* with *o'clock*.

O'clock

It's ten past five.
~~*It's ten past five o'clock.*~~

I'll see you at a quarter past three.
~~*I'll see you at a quarter past three o'clock.*~~

You use *o'clock* only when saying exact hours, not times between hours. Compare these sentences:

*It's **two o'clock**.*
*It's **half past five**.*

Note that when writing *o'clock* people usually write the number before it as a word and not as a figure.

Today/tonight

I'm seeing her later today.
~~*I'm seeing her later this day.*~~

We're going out tonight.
~~*We're going out this night.*~~

Remember that you say *today* and *tonight*. You do not say *this day* or *this night*.

By

We'll be finished by three.

Total sales reached 1 million by 2010.

~~*We'll be finished until three.*~~

~~*Total sales reached 1 million until 2010.*~~

If something happens before or at a particular time, you say it happens *by* that time. Do not use *until* for this.

For

> I went to Madrid for two weeks.
> ~~I went to Madrid during two weeks.~~

> We've been married for seven years.
> ~~We've been married since seven years.~~

Use *for*, and not *during* or *since*, when you are stating a period of time (*the weekend, three weeks, two years*, etc.) in which something happens or is true.

From

> He was the headmaster here from 1998 to 2007.
>
> ~~He was the headmaster here since 1998 to 2007.~~

> The noise continued from nine in the morning till ten o'clock at night.
>
> ~~The noise continued since nine in the morning till ten o'clock at night.~~

To say when something began and finished, use *from* and *to/till/until*.
Do not use *since* and *to/till/until*.

On

> I was born on March 11th.
> ~~I was born in March 11th.~~

> On Tuesday, I went shopping.
> ~~In Tuesday, I went shopping.~~

Do not say that something happens *in* a particular day or date. Say that it happens *on* that day or date.

Since

> We've lived here since 2005.
>
> ~~We've lived here from 2005.~~

> I've been doing art classes since February.
>
> ~~I've been doing art classes from February.~~

Use *since* and not *from* to say that something began to happen at a particular time in the past and is still happening now.

Note that in sentences like these, you must use a present perfect form:

> I **haven't eaten** meat **since** I was twelve.
> I**'ve been wearing** glasses **since** I was three.

At night

> They worked from seven in the morning until ten at night.
> ~~They worked from seven in the morning until ten in the night.~~

> There were no lights in the street at night.
> ~~There were no lights in the street in the night.~~

You say *in the morning*, *in the afternoon*, and *in the evening*, but note that you say *at night*.

Last month/week, etc.

> Last summer we went to the US.
> ~~The last summer we went to the US.~~

> I saw her last Saturday.
> ~~I saw her the last Saturday.~~

When you put *last* before a word such as *week*, *month*, or *Tuesday* to say when something happened, do not use the article *the* before it.

The last few weeks/the last eight days

> The last few weeks have been really difficult.
> ~~The few last weeks have been really difficult.~~

> We've made a lot of progress in the last three days.
> ~~We've made a lot of progress in the three last days.~~

Note the order of the words in these examples. *Last* always comes before words such as *few*, *eight*, etc.

Yesterday morning/afternoon/evening

> The parcel arrived yesterday morning.
> ~~The parcel arrived last morning.~~

> Yesterday afternoon, I had lunch with Melissa.
> ~~Last afternoon, I had lunch with Melissa.~~

Say *yesterday morning* and *yesterday afternoon*, and not ~~last morning~~ and ~~last afternoon~~. *Yesterday evening* is possible, but people generally refer to this as *last night*. Note that ~~yesterday night~~ is never said. This is always *last night*:

> Sara called to tell me the news **last night**.
> I didn't sleep so well **last night**.

The previous night, etc./the night, etc. before

I saw Ben on Tuesday. He said he'd seen
    Greg the previous evening.
~~I saw Ben on Tuesday. He said he'd seen
    Greg the last evening.~~

We spoke about a film that we'd
    seen the night before.
~~We spoke about a film that we'd
    seen the last night.~~

When you are describing something that happened in the past and you
want to refer to an earlier period of time, say the previous day/evening/night,
etc., or the day/evening/night, etc. before. Do not use the word last.

Next week/Thursday, etc.

I'm going away next week.
~~I'm going away the next week.~~

He'll be 70 next April.
~~He'll be 70 in the next April.~~

Do not use the or a preposition in front of next.

Note that the day after today is tomorrow and never *next day*. Similarly,
do not say that something will happen *next morning*, *next afternoon*, *next
evening*, or *next night*. Use tomorrow morning, tomorrow afternoon, tomorrow
evening, and tomorrow night.

Lasts/takes two hours/three minutes, etc.

Each song lasts ten minutes.

~~Each song lasts ten minutes' time.~~

The whole process takes two or
    more years.
~~The whole process takes two or
    more years' time.~~

You do not use the word time when you are using words such as minutes,
hours, years, etc. to say how long something lasts or takes. Note, however,
that you can use time when you are saying how long it will be before
something happens:

We're getting married in **three months' time**.
It should all be ready in **a few days' time**.

A long time

I spent a long time cleaning this room.

~~I spent long time cleaning this room.~~

It takes a long time to learn
a language properly.

~~It takes long time to learn
a language properly.~~

Remember that when you use an adjective before the word *time*, for example *a long time*, you must use *a* before the whole phrase.

On time or in time?

Trains here always arrive on time.

~~Trains here always arrive in time.~~

We got there just in time to see the
start of the film.

~~We got there just on time to see the
start of the film.~~

Be careful not to confuse *on time* and *in time*. If something happens *on time*, it happens at the right time or punctually. If you are *in time* for a particular event, you are not late for it.

Travel

Arrive

We arrived in London at nine o'clock.

We arrived to London at nine o'clock.

We finally arrived at the coach station.

We finally arrived in the coach station.

You *arrive at* a place, such as a station, airport, etc. and you *arrive in* a country or city. You never *arrive to* a place or a country or city. Note also that you do not use a preposition between the word *arrive* and the words *home*, *here*, *there*, *somewhere*, or *anywhere*:

*We **arrived home** just after midnight.*
*I **arrived here** yesterday.*
*We'd only just **arrived there**.*

Reach

It was dark by the time I reached John's apartment.

It was dark by the time I reached at John's apartment.

They texted me when they reached Portland.

They texted me when they reached.

Reach always takes a direct object. Do not say that someone *reaches at* a place or that someone just *reaches*.

Arrival

On your arrival, please report to the visitors' office.

At your arrival, please report to the visitors' office.

On his arrival, he went straight to the hotel.

At his arrival, he went straight to the hotel.

If you want to say that something happens immediately after someone arrives at a place, you can say it happens *on/upon their arrival*. Note that this is a slightly formal phrase. Do not say *at their arrival*.

Travel/journey/trip/voyage

I'm going away on a business trip.

We had to do quite a long car journey.

~~I'm going away on a business travel.~~

~~We had to do quite a long car travel.~~

Travel, meaning 'the act of travelling' is uncountable. Do not say ~~a travel~~. Instead, use *a journey*, *a trip* or, less commonly (on a ship), *a voyage*:

We're going on a **day trip** to the seaside.
On long **journeys**, Emily often gets sick.
It was the ship's second **voyage**.

Note that you do not use the verb *do* with any of these nouns. You *make* or *go on* a journey, you *take* or *go on* a trip, and you *make* a voyage:

He **made** the long **journey** to India.
We **took** a bus **trip** to Oxford.
The ship **made** the 4,000-kilometre **voyage** across the Atlantic.

By bicycle/car/coach, etc.

I never go by car.

It's cheaper to travel by coach.

~~I never go by a car.~~

~~It's cheaper to travel by a coach.~~

You can use *by* with most forms of transport when you are talking about travel using that form of transport, but do not use a determiner after *by*.

Note also that you can only say simply *by car/coach/train*, etc. if you are saying nothing more about the car, etc. For example, you cannot use *by* instead of *in* and *on* in these sentences:

I came **in** Tom's car.
I travelled a lot **on** public buses in Chengdu.

Age

Be + number

I'm 26.
~~I have 26.~~

He's only six.
~~He only has six.~~

To say how old someone is, use the verb *be* followed by a number. Do not use the verb *have* to talk about age.

Five-month-old baby/nineteen-year-old student, etc.

a six-year-old boy
~~a six-years-old boy~~

a thirty-two-year-old man
~~a thirty-two-years-old man~~

You can mention someone's age using a compound adjective in front of a noun. Note that the noun referring to the period of time, such as *year* or *month*, is always singular whatever the number.

A man of about 60

He was with a woman of about thirty.

~~He was with a woman about thirty.~~

He was a small thin man of about fifty.

~~He was a small thin man about fifty.~~

Do not use *about*, *almost*, or *nearly* immediately after a noun. Use *of* immediately after the noun and then *about*, *almost*, or *nearly*.

Saying how old something is

Our house is about a hundred years old.
~~Our house is about a hundred.~~

We have a ten-year-old car.
~~We have a car that is ten.~~

To describe the age of something, you cannot just use *be* and a number, as you do for a person. However, you can use *be* and a number, plus the phrase *years old*:

Our sofa **is** over **thirty years old**.

You can also use a compound adjective in front of the noun. Again, note that the noun referring to the period of time, such as *year* or *month* is always singular:

I have a **twenty-year-old** bike.

Meals

Have breakfast/lunch/dinner

We had breakfast and then left.
~~We had a breakfast and then left.~~

I had lunch at 1:00.
~~I had the lunch at 1:00.~~

You say that someone *has breakfast/lunch*, etc. Do not say that someone ~~has a breakfast/lunch~~, etc. or that someone ~~has the breakfast/lunch~~, etc.

Note that you use *a* before a meal if you are using an adjective to describe that meal:

We had **a quiet dinner** together.
We had **a quick breakfast** and then left.

Make breakfast/lunch/dinner

I'll go and make dinner.

~~I'll go and make a dinner.~~

On Sundays Tom makes the breakfast.

~~On Sundays Tom makes a breakfast.~~

When someone prepares a meal, you say that they *make breakfast/dinner*, etc. You can also say that they *make the breakfast/dinner*, etc. or that they *make their breakfast/dinner*, etc. Do not say that they ~~make a breakfast/dinner~~, etc.

Colours

Be + red/blue/white, etc.

What colour was the scarf?

His eyes were the colour of the ocean.

~~*What colour has the scarf?*~~

~~*His eyes had the colour of the ocean.*~~

You say that something *is* a particular colour. Do not say that something *has* a particular colour.

A green sweater/a red dress, etc.

She's wearing a green sweater.

He was wearing a dark blue jacket.

~~*She's wearing a green colour sweater.*~~

~~*He was wearing a dark blue colour jacket.*~~

When you are describing the colour of something, you do not usually use the word *colour*. Note, however, that you do use the word *colour* to ask about the colour of something:

*What **colour** is your car?*

A beautiful, red, silk shirt

He pointed to a small, white, wooden house.

She was wearing a pretty, pink woollen scarf.

~~*He pointed to a white, small, wooden house.*~~

~~*She was wearing a woollen, pretty, pink scarf.*~~

When more than one adjective is used before a noun and one of them is a colour adjective, the usual rules for where the colour adjective goes are as follows:

1. Adjectives showing a quality, eg *sad, tall, clever* ('qualitative adjectives')
2. Colour adjectives
3. Adjectives showing that something is of a particular type, eg *wooden, daily, financial* ('classifying adjectives')

Speaking

Discuss

I discussed it with him.
~~I discussed with him.~~

We discussed what to do about the problem.
~~We discussed.~~

Discuss is always followed by a direct object, a wh- clause, or a whether- clause. Do not use it without one of these.

Say

She said that Charlie had left.
~~She said me that Charlie had left.~~

I told her that I liked her dress.
~~I said her that I liked her dress.~~

Do not use say with an indirect object. Use a that- clause after it, or use the verb tell with the indirect object instead.

Note also that if you are using say to report the general meaning of what you or someone said, rather than the actual words, use so and not it:

I disagreed with him and I **said so**.

I know she liked it because she **said so**.

Speak

Leonie is from the Netherlands so she speaks Dutch.
~~Leonie is from the Netherlands so she speaks in Dutch.~~

Luisa is from Spain so she speaks Spanish.
~~Luisa is from Spain so she is speaking Spanish.~~

When you are talking about someone's ability to speak a language, say that they speak a language. Do not say that they speak in a language. Also, do not say that someone is speaking a language to mean that they are able to speak that language.

Suggest

I suggested that we leave.
~~I suggested her that we leave.~~

He suggested to me that we should go by train.
~~He suggested me that we should go by train.~~

Suggest is not usually followed by a noun or pronoun referring to a person. You usually have to put the preposition to between the verb and the noun/pronoun. You can also suggest that someone does something.

Talk

They sat in the kitchen, drinking tea
and talking.

~~They sat in the kitchen, drinking tea
and speaking.~~

He talked about his business.

~~He said about his business.~~

If two or more people are having a conversation, you usually say that they are *talking* and not *speaking*.

Do not use *say about* to mention what subject someone is speaking about. Use *talk about*.

Tell

He told me that he was a doctor.

~~He told to me that he was a doctor.~~

I told him that I was leaving.

~~I told to him that I was leaving.~~

When you use the verb *tell*, do not put the preposition *to* before the indirect object.

Note also that if you are using *tell* to report the general meaning of what you or someone said, rather than the actual words, use *so* and not *it*:

I know they're leaving because they **told** me **so**.

Tell a joke/lie/story

You're telling lies now.

~~You're saying lies now.~~

Come on, tell us a joke!

~~Come on, say us a joke!~~

You say that someone *tells* a joke, a lie, or a story. You do not say that they *say* a joke, a lie, or a story.

Spelling

General spelling rules

Adding a suffix to words that end with a silent -e

I'm hoping to see him later.
~~I'm hopeing to see him later.~~

The mark was very noticeable.
~~The mark was very noticable.~~

When you add a suffix that begins with a vowel, you drop the -e:

abbreviate + -ion = abbreviation
desire + -able = desirable

Be careful, though. If the word ends in -ce and sounds like s, or the word ends in -ge and sounds like j, you do not drop the final -e:

change + -able = changeable
outrage + -ous = outrageous

Adding a suffix to words that end with a consonant

They were running away.
~~They were runing away.~~

He has committed several crimes.
~~He has commited several crimes.~~

In words of one syllable ending in a short vowel plus a consonant, you double the final consonant when you add a suffix that begins with a vowel:

thin + -est = thinnest
swim + -er = swimmer

In words of more than one syllable ending in a single vowel plus a consonant, if the stress is on the end of the word when it is pronounced, you double the final consonant when you add a suffix that begins with a vowel:

begin + -ing = beginning
occur + -ence = occurrence

When you add a suffix that begins with a vowel to a word that ends in a single vowel plus *l* or *p*, you double the *l* or *p*:

cancel + -ation = cancellation
wrap + -ing = wrapping

Note that in US English, the *l* is not usually doubled.

Spelling 155

When you add a suffix that begins with *e-*, *i-* or *y-* to a word that ends in *-c*, you add a *k* after the *c*. This is to keep the hard *k* sound when it is pronounced:

mimic + -ed = mimicked
panic + -y = panicky

Adding a suffix to words that end with -y

The flowers were beautiful. *It gave us great happiness.*
~~*The flowers were beautyful.*~~ ~~*It gave us great happyness.*~~

When you add a suffix to a word that ends with a consonant plus *y*, you change the *y* to *i*:

crazy + -ly = crazily
lonely + -ness = loneliness

Be careful though, there are a few words that do not follow this rule. The most common one is *shy*:

shy + -ly = shyly

Words ending in -*ful*

The cut was really painful. *He was a faithful friend.*
~~*The cut was really painfull.*~~ ~~*He was a faithfull friend.*~~

You always spell the suffix *-ful* with just one *l*.

Words beginning with *al-*

I've already spoken to her. *That's £5.50 altogether.*
~~*I've allready spoken to her.*~~ ~~*That's £5.50 alltogether.*~~

When *all* and another word are joined to make a word without a hyphen, you drop the second *l*.

Words ending with -ic

The labels are printed automatically.   *We clapped enthusiastically.*
~~The labels are printed automaticly.~~   *~~We clapped enthusiasticly.~~*

To make an adjective that ends in -ic into an adverb, you must add -ally, not just -ly.

-ie- *or* -ei-?

We have achieved a lot this week.   *We painted the ceiling white.*
~~We have acheived a lot this week.~~   *~~We painted the cieling white.~~*

The phrase '*i before e except after c*' is a useful phrase to learn. It means that when *i* and *e* are put together to make the sound '*ee*', the *i* comes before the *e*, for example in words like *brief*, *relief*, and *chief*.

However, when they follow the letter *c* in a word, the *e* comes before the *i*, for example in words such as *receipt*, *receive*, and *deceive*.

Note that there are several words that do not follow this rule. There are two other rules you can learn. In words like *neighbour* and *weight*, where the *ie* sound is pronounced /eɪ/, the spelling is *ei*. In words like *ancient* and *efficient*, where the *cie* sound is pronounced /ʃə/, the spelling is *ie*.

There are a few words, for example *caffeine*, *protein*, and *seize*, that do not follow any of these rules, and must be learned individually.

Words that are often spelled incorrectly

People often make spelling mistakes with the following words:

accidentally	Don't forget -ally at the end, not just -ly.
accommodation	Double c and double m. This is one of the most commonly misspelled words in English.
acquire	Don't forget the c before the q.
address	Double d and double s.
advertisement	Don't forget the e after the s.

apparent	Double *p* but only one *r*.
beautiful	Learn the group of vowels *eau* at the beginning.
because	Remember *au* after the *c*.
believe	Remember *ie*, not *ei*.
Britain	Don't forget the *i* in the second syllable.
business	The first vowel is *u*, and don't forget the *i* in the middle.
catastrophe	Unusually for English, the final *-e* is pronounced, but remember it is only one *e* – don't be tempted to write *-y* or *-ee*.
category	Remember it's *e* in the middle, not *i* or *a*.
colleague	Don't forget the *-ue* at the end.
debt	Don't forget the silent *b*.
definite/ definitely	Remember that there are two *i*'s and no *a* in this word.
different	Double *f* and don't forget the *e* after them.
discipline	Don't forget the *c* after the *s* or the *-e* at the end.
doubt	Don't forget the silent *b*.
embarrassing	Double *r* and double *s*.
encyclopaedia *or* encyclopedia	Formerly, UK English used the first of these spellings, but the second is now used commonly. US English uses *encyclopedia*.
environment	Don't forget the *n* in the middle of this word.
especially	Remember that this word starts with *e-*.
existence	This word ends *-ence*, not *-ance*.

favourite	Don't forget the *u* in the middle of this word. However, in US English, this word is spelled *favorite*.
foreign	Remember *ei* in the second syllable, and don't forget the *g*.
forty	Unlike *four*, there is no *u* in this word.
friend	Remember the vowel sound is written *ie*.
government	Don't forget the *n* in the middle of this word. Remember that it comes from the verb *govern*.
grammar	Remember that this word ends -*ar*, not -*er*.
guarantee	Remember the *u* in the first syllable of this word.
guess	Don't forget the *u*.
guilty	Don't forget the *u*.
height	The vowel is *ei*, and don't forget the -*gh* at the end.
immediately	Don't forget the double *m*.
independent	Remember that this word ends -*ent*, not -*ant*.
island	Don't forget the silent *s*.
jealous	Don't forget the *a* in the first vowel.
jewellery	In UK English, don't forget the double *l* and the *e* before -*ry*.
leisure	Remember that in this word, *e* comes before *i*, which is the other way round from the usual rule.
library	Don't forget the *r* after the *b*.
lightning	Don't be tempted to add an *e* after *light*.

manoeuvre	The British spelling of this word (both the noun and the verb) has the complicated set of vowels -oeu- in it. The US English spelling of this word is *maneuver*.
mediaeval *or* **medieval**	Formerly, UK English used the first of these spellings, but the second is now used commonly. US English uses *medieval*.
millennium	Double *l* and double *n*.
miniature	Don't forget the second *i*.
minuscule	Note that the second vowel is *u*, not *i*. Try to think of it as beginning with *minus-*, not *mini-*.
necessary	Remember one *c* and double *s*.
niece	The vowels are *ie*.
occurrence	Double *c* and double *r*.
opportunity	Double *p* and don't forget the *r* before the *t*.
parliament	Don't forget the *i* in the second syllable.
possess/possession	Two lots of double *s*.
privilege	Remember that the middle vowel is *i*, and the last vowel is *-e*. There are no *a*'s in this word.
profession/ professional/ professor	Remember there is only one *f* in these words.
pronunciation	Don't be tempted to add an *o* in the second syllable.
questionnaire	Remember to write double *n* in the middle.
queue	Don't forget double *ue*.
receipt	Remember *ei* in the second syllable, and don't forget the silent *p*.

receive	Remember *ei* in the second syllable.
recommend	Only one *c* but double *m*.
relevant	Remember that the second vowel is *e*, not *a*.
restaurant	Remember to write *au* after the first *t*.
rhythm	Remember the silent *h* at the beginning and the vowel is *y*. There is no vowel in the second syllable.
seize	Remember *ei*, here not *ie*.
separate	Remember that the second vowel is *a*, not *e*.
temporary	Remember the *a* before -*ry*.
truly	Don't be tempted to add an *e* after *tru*-.
vegetable	Remember the *e* after *veg*-.
vehicle	Remember the *h*.
Wednesday	Remember the *d* in the first syllable.
weird	Remember *ei*, not *ie*.

Punctuation

This section covers common mistakes connected with punctuation. For a full explanation of how to use punctuation marks, look in a grammar book or a usage book.

Apostrophes [']

For possession

That is John's jacket.
That is Johns jacket.

I've got the children's tickets.
I've got the childrens tickets.

The apostrophe is used to show that something belongs to someone. It is usually added to the end of a word and followed by an -s.

Not for plurals

I'd like five tomatoes.
I'd like five tomato's.

The food is for the boys.
The food is for the boy's.

Do not use an apostrophe to make plurals.

For contracted forms

The door won't open.
The door wont open.

He's lost his keys.
Hes lost his keys.

An apostrophe is used in shortened forms of words to show that one or more letters have been missed out. Do not leave out the apostrophe.

Commas [,]

For long sentences
(→ p.104 see also: commas in defining clauses)

The comma marks a short pause between parts of a sentence.

Commas are normally used if the subordinate clause (the part of the sentence that is not the main part) comes before the main clause:

If you have any problems, just call me.
Just call me if you have any problems.

Sometimes a comma is used even when the main clause comes first, if the clauses are particularly long:

We should be able to finish the work by the end of the week, if nothing unexpected turns up between now and then.

For lists

You will need pens, paper, and calculators.
~~You will need pens paper and calculators.~~

We had fish and rice for lunch.
~~We had fish, and rice for lunch.~~

Commas are used to separate three or more items in a list or series. Do not use a comma when there are only two items.

Note that the comma is often not given before the final *and* or *or*:

They breed dogs, cats, rabbits and hamsters.
We did canoeing, climbing and archery.

Between adjectives

It was a hot, dry and dusty road.
~~It was a hot dry and dusty road.~~

It was a long and difficult journey.
~~It was a long, and difficult journey.~~

If you use more than one adjective, put a comma between them. However, do not put a comma if the adjectives are linked with *and* or *or*.

Question marks [?]

For direct and indirect questions

The lady said, 'Where are you going?'

The lady asked where she was going.

~~The lady said, 'Where are you going.'~~

~~The lady asked where she was going?~~

You should always use question marks in direct questions, i.e. when the actual words of a speaker are used. A reported question should end with a full stop.

Quotation marks [' ' *or* " "]

For writing speech

'I'm Harry,' he said.

~~'I'm Harry', he said.~~

'Do I know you?' she asked.

~~'Do I know you'? she asked.~~

You should always put quotation marks around the actual words that a speaker uses. In UK English, you can use single (' ') or double (" ") quotation marks. In US English, double quotation marks are more common.

The comma, question mark, or exclamation mark comes inside the quotation marks, unless you put the reporting verb in the middle of a sentence that does not have punctuation itself:

'There is', Monica said, 'nothing we can do about it.'

Capital letters

I have Spanish classes every
    Wednesday.
~~I have spanish classes every~~
    ~~wednesday.~~

He reads The Times every day.

~~He reads the times every day.~~

Remember to use capital letters for the following:

the first word in a sentence, eg *Dinner will be at twelve.*
the first person pronoun *I*, eg *I hope you like pizza.*
proper names, eg *Jane Smith*, *Lord Owen*
days of the week, eg *Monday*, *Saturday*
months of the year, eg *December*, *August*
public holidays, eg *Christmas*, *Yom Kippur*
nationalities, eg *Spanish*, *Iraqi*
languages, eg *Swahili*, *Japanese*
geographical locations, eg *Australia*, *Mount Everest*, *The Indian Ocean*
company names, eg *Starbucks*, *Visa*
the first word and the main words in titles of books, films, etc.,
    eg *Twelfth Night*, *The Secret Garden*

Exercises
and
Solutions

Verbs

Prepositions after verbs

A. Complete the sentences by choosing the correct preposition from the word pool to follow each verb.

> **on   about   with   to   for   of**

1. He accused me .... lying to him.

2. I apologised .... getting her name wrong.

3. You're not listening .... me, Ethan!

4. I agree .... Robin that we need to take on more staff.

5. We mainly talked .... work.

6. That's her main source of income and she relies .... it.

Verb + *to-* infinitive *or* verb + *-ing*?

B. Complete the sentences by circling the correct form of the verb.

1. I can't afford to *buy / buying* a bike at the moment.

2. She came into the room and I pretended *being / to be* asleep.

3. Isobel was planning her day in London and I suggested *going / to go* to the Natural History Museum.

4. Did you manage to *fit / fitting* all the luggage in your car?

5. We considered *going / to go* to France for our holidays.

6. Sometimes I enjoy *to be / being* on my own for a few hours.

Tenses

Present simple *or* present progressive?

A. Complete the sentences by writing the present simple or the present progressive form of the verb in brackets.

1. I .... (*study*) to be a lawyer.

2. I .... (*walk*) along the same street every day.

3. Can I call you back, Dan? I .... (*have*) dinner at the moment.

4. In the evening, I usually .... (*watch*) TV or

    .... (*see*) my friends.

5. It .... (*feel*) strange to be back in the office where I used to work.

6. I .... (*work*) in Paris for a year.

Present perfect *or* past simple?

B. Complete the sentences by circling the correct form of the verb.

1. She *has left / left* for New York yesterday.

2. You must be hungry. It's six o'clock now and you *didn't eat / haven't eaten* all day.

3. I'm a bit worried about Luke. I *haven't heard / didn't hear* from him since last weekend.

4. I *had / have had* dinner with Gemma last week.

5. I'm tired! I *have got up / got up* at 4 o'clock this morning.

6. I don't know what Jane thinks about the situation. I *haven't spoken / didn't speak* to her yet.

Nouns

Article *or* no article?

A. Look at the nouns in **bold** in these sentences and consider whether they need articles before them. Which sentences are correct?

1. Children in these countries start **school** when they are seven.

2. He was found guilty and sent to the **prison**.

3. When I'm older, I hope to go to **university**.

4. We don't have anything for dinner so I'll go to the **supermarket** on my way home.

5. We went for a walk after **dinner**.

6. The **poverty** is a serious problem.

Which determiner?

B. Complete the sentences by circling the correct determiner.

1. There were too *many / much* people there and the room was really crowded.

2. Could I have *another / other* glass of wine, please?

3. Nearly *every / each* person in the room was wearing jeans.

4. I must have seen fifteen or sixteen jackets and I didn't like *none / any* of them.

5. She gave me too *much / many* pasta and I couldn't eat all of it.

6. In *other / another* towns, they have better transport systems.

Adjectives

-ed or *-ing*?

Complete the sentences by forming an adjective from the verb in brackets. Use either an adjective ending in *-ed* or an adjective ending in *-ing*.

1. Her sudden death in a car crash was very .... (*shock*).

2. I'm afraid I found the film incredibly .... (*bore*).

3. I was a bit .... (*surprise*) that she didn't want to go to the party.

4. It was a really .... (*interest*) article.

5. Don't be .... (*frighten*)! The dog won't harm you!

6. I'm so .... (*excite*) about my party tomorrow!

Adverbs

Adverbs formed from adjectives

Complete the sentences by forming an adverb from the adjective in brackets.

1. Ella did really .... (*good*) in her exams.

2. I had to run really .... (*fast*) to get to the station on time.

3. They waited .... (*patient*) in the rain for the concert to start.

4. We both work really .... (*hard*).

5. Remember to set off .... (*early*).

6. I'll .... (*easy*) get to the restaurant for seven o'clock.

Pronouns

Which pronoun?

Complete the sentences by choosing the correct pronoun from the word pool.

> **neither**   **her**   **anything**   **any**   **herself**   **anyone**

1. I didn't know .... at the party so I had nobody to speak to.

2. My little sister fell off her bike and hurt ....

3. She asked me to lend her some money so I gave .... twenty dollars.

4. You need some food, Sophie. You haven't had .... to eat since breakfast.

5. We looked at two apartments but, unfortunately, ... was suitable.

6. I need some chocolate for this recipe. Do we have ....?

Prepositions

Which preposition?

Are the **bold** prepositions correct or incorrect in these sentences?

1. I would think he's **round** thirty.

2. He works **as** a teacher in the local school.

3. Which cities did you visit **except** Oxford and Bath?

4. I sat **between** Richard and his wife.

5. I went to New York **during** three days.

6. My brother owns **over** twenty pairs of trainers.

Sentences

Question tags

A. Change these statements into questions by adding question tags, such as *isn't it*, *aren't you*, *don't they*, etc.

1. This food is delicious, ...?

2. You've been to Venice, Melissa, ...?

3. You like silent movies, ...?

4. He doesn't speak English, ...?

5. We replied to the invitation, ...?

6. You're not going to the party, ...?

Conditionals

B. Complete these conditional sentences by circling the correct structure.

1. Metal expands when it *will get / gets* hotter.

2. If it *is / will be* a nice day tomorrow, we'll go to the beach.

3. If I *had / would have* more time, I would go travelling.

4. I would buy a better car if I *would earn / earned* more money.

5. If I'd known you were in town, I would *have invited / invite* you.

6. Of course, it would have been better if I *would have / had* told James the truth.

Collocations

C. Complete these sentences by using the correct form of the verbs *make* or *do*.

1. I'll come out when I've .... my homework.

2. I really wasn't enjoying the party, so I .... an excuse and left.

3. All parents want to hear that their child is .... good progress in their subjects at school.

4. They've .... a lot of research into this area.

5. She has .... a lot of friends since starting school.

6. I keep telling her she needs to .... more of an effort to meet people.

Which Words?

Correct or incorrect words?

Complete the sentences by circling the correct word.

1. It's George's *anniversary / birthday* today. He's six years old!

2. You look great in red, Lucy. It really *suits / fits* you.

3. Lovely to see you, Sam! Let me *buy / pay* you a drink.

4. It's a disgrace that the company still has no *feminine / female* directors.

5. I suddenly *understood / realized* that I hadn't invited Polly to the party.

6. You shouldn't have to *put up with / support* that sort of rudeness from a member of staff.

Confusable Words

Correct or incorrect words?

Are the **bold** words correct or incorrect in these sentences?

1. You can't go out in winter with **bear** legs!

2. The driver of the truck claimed that the crash was caused by his **breaks** failing.

3. Her **role** at work is to manage the project.

4. Ian ate the **hole** cake!

5. They forgot to bring **there** tickets.

6. Sarah's a very **sensible** child. I can trust her not to do anything silly.

Spelling

General spelling rules

Complete the sentences by changing the parts of speech of the words in brackets. Make sure you use the general spelling rules to do this.

1. This cut on my hand is really .... (*pain*).

2. It was so hard being away from all her family and friends. The .... (*lonely*) was terrible.

3. I said hello to the little girl and she smiled .... (*shy*).

4. He eventually found .... (*happy*) with his second wife and they had three children.

5. We clapped .... (*enthusiastic*) at the end of the performance.

6. A small boy skipped .... (*happy*) along the street.

Solutions

Verbs

A: 1 of 2 for 3 to 4 with 5 about 6 on
B: 1 to buy 2 to be 3 going 4 to fit 5 going 6 being

Tenses

A: 1 am studying 2 walk 3 am having 4 watch, see 5 feels
6 am working
B: 1 left 2 haven't eaten 3 haven't heard 4 had 5 got up
6 haven't spoken

Nouns

A: 1 correct 2 incorrect 3 correct 4 correct 5 correct 6 incorrect
B: 1 many 2 another 3 every 4 any 5 much 6 other

Adjectives

1 shocking 2 boring 3 surprised 4 interesting 5 frightened 6 excited

Adverbs

1 well 2 fast 3 patiently 4 hard 5 early 6 easily

Pronouns

1 anyone 2 herself 3 her 4 anything 5 neither 6 any

Prepositions

1 incorrect (about/around) 2 correct 3 incorrect (besides) 4 correct
5 incorrect (for) 6 correct

Sentences

A: 1 isn't it 2 haven't you 3 don't you 4 does he 5 didn't we 6 are you
B: 1 gets 2 is 3 had 4 earned 5 have invited 6 had
C: 1 done 2 made 3 making 4 done 5 made 6 make

Which Word?

A: 1 birthday 2 suits 3 buy 4 female 5 realized 6 put up with

Confusable Words

A: 1 incorrect (bare) 2 incorrect (brakes) 3 correct 4 incorrect (whole)
5 incorrect (their) 6 correct

Spelling

A: 1 painful 2 loneliness 3 shyly 4 happiness 5 enthusiastically
6 happily

Glossary

adjective a word used to tell you more about a person or thing, such as their appearance, colour, size, or other qualities; eg ...*a **pretty blue** dress*.

adverb a word that gives more information about when, how, where, or in what circumstances something happens; eg *quickly, now*.

adverbial phrase two or more words that function as an adverb; eg *so well*

article either of the words 'a' or 'the' that are used before nouns.

auxiliary verb one of the verbs 'be', 'have', and 'do' when they are used with a main verb to form tenses, negatives, and questions.

base form the form of a verb without any endings added to it; eg *walk, go, have, be*.

clause a group of words containing a verb.

collective noun a noun that refers to a group of people or things, which can be used with a singular or plural verb; eg *committee, team, family*.

comparative an adjective or adverb with '-er' on the end or 'more' in front of it; eg *slower, more important, more carefully*.

conditional a conditional clause usually starts with 'if' or 'unless', and is used to talk about possible situations and their results; eg *They would be rich **if they had taken** my advice*... *We'll go to the park, **unless it rains***.

conjunction a word such as 'and', 'because', or 'nor', that links two clauses, groups, or words.

consonant a sound such as 'p', 'f', 'n', or 't' which you pronounce by stopping the air flowing freely through your mouth.

countable noun a noun which has both singular and plural forms; eg *dog/dogs, foot/feet lemon/lemons*.

defining relative clause a relative clause which identifies the person or thing that is being talked about; eg ...*the lady **who lives next door***... *I wrote down everything **that she said***.

determiner one of a group of words including 'the', 'a', 'some', and 'my', which are used at the beginning of a noun group.

direct object a noun group referring to the person or thing affected by an action, in a clause with a verb in the active voice; eg *She wrote **her name**... I shut **the windows***.

indefinite pronoun a small group of pronouns including 'someone' and 'anything' which are used to refer to people or things without saying exactly who or what they are.

indirect object an object used with verbs that take two objects. For example, in 'I gave him the pen' and 'I gave the pen to him', 'him' is the indirect object.

indirect question a question used to ask for information or help; eg *Do you know **where Jane is**?*

infinitive the base form of a verb; eg *I wanted to **go**... She helped me **dig** the garden*. The infinitive is the form you look up in a dictionary.

'-ing' form a verb form ending in '-ing' which is used to form verb tenses, and as an adjective or a noun.

intransitive verb a verb which does not take an object; eg *She **arrived**... I **was yawning***.

irregular verb a verb that has three or five forms, or whose forms do not follow the normal rules.

link verb a verb which takes a complement rather than an object; eg *be, become, seem, appear*.

modal a verb such as 'can', 'might', or 'will', which is used to express concepts such as requests, offers, suggestions, possibility, or certainty.

negative a negative clause, question, sentence, or statement is one which has a negative word such as 'not', and indicates the absence or opposite of something, or is used to say that something is not the case; eg *I **don't** know you... I'll **never** forget*.

non-defining relative clause a relative clause which gives more information about someone or something, but which is not needed to identify them because we already know who or what they are; eg *That's Mary, **who was at university with me***.

object a noun group which refers to a person or thing that is affected by the action described by a verb or preposition.

object pronoun one of a set of pronouns including 'me', 'him', and 'them', which are used as the object of a verb or preposition.

participle a verb form used for making different tenses. Verbs have two participles, a present participle and a past participle.

particle an adverb or preposition which combines with verbs to form phrasal verbs.

passive the passive is formed with 'be' and the past participle of the verb. In a passive clause, the subject of the verb is the person or thing that is affected by the action.

past participle a verb form which is used to form perfect tenses and passives. Some past participles are also used as adjectives; eg *watched, broken*.

past perfect the past perfect tense is formed with 'had' with a past participle and is used to refer to past events; eg *She **had finished** her meal*.

personal pronoun one of the group of words including 'I', 'you', and 'me', which are used to refer back to yourself, the people you are talking to, or the people or things you are talking about.

phrasal verb a combination of a verb and a particle, which together have a different meaning to the verb on its own; eg *back down, hand over, look forward to*.

plural the form of a count noun or verb, which is used to refer to or talk about more than one person or thing; eg ***Dogs have ears**... The **women were** outside*.

possessive pronoun one of the pronouns 'mine', 'yours', 'hers', 'his', 'ours', or 'theirs'.

preposition a word such as 'by', 'with' or 'from', which is always followed by a noun group.

prepositional phrase a structure consisting of a preposition followed by a noun group as its object; eg *on the table, by the sea*.

present perfect the present perfect tense is formed with 'have' or 'has' with a past participle and is used to refer to past events which exist in the present; eg *She **has loved** him for over ten years*.

progressive tense a tense which contains a form of the verb 'be' and a present participle; eg *She **was laughing**... They **had been playing** badminton*.

pronoun a word which you use instead of a noun, when you do not need or want to name someone or something directly; eg *it, you, none*.

quantifier a word or phrase which is used to refer to a quantity of something without being precise; eg *plenty, a lot*

question tag an auxiliary or modal with a pronoun, which is used to turn a statement into a question. eg *He's very friendly, **isn't he**?... I can come, **can't I**?*

reflexive pronoun a pronoun ending in '-self' or '-selves', such as 'myself' or 'themselves', which you use as the object of a verb when you want to say that the object is the same person or thing as the subject of the verb in the same clause; eg *He hurt **himself**.*

reflexive verb a verb which is normally used with a reflexive pronoun as object; eg *He **contented himself** with the thought that he had the only set of keys to the car.*

relative clause a clause which gives more information about someone or something mentioned in the main clause.

relative pronoun 'that' or a 'wh-' word such as 'who' or 'which', when it is used to introduce a relative clause; eg *...the girl **who** was carrying the bag.*

reporting verb a verb that is used to show that someone is speaking; eg *say, tell, describe*

simple tense a present or past tense formed without using an auxiliary verb; eg *...I **wait**. ...she **sang**.*

singular the form of a count noun or verb which is used to refer to or talk about one person or thing; eg *A **dog was** in the **car**... That **woman is** my **mother**.*

subject the noun group in a clause that refers to the person or thing who does the action expressed by the verb; eg ***We** were going shopping.*

subject pronoun one of the set of pronouns including 'I', 'she', and 'they', which are used as the subject of a verb.

suffix a letter or group of letters which is added to the end of a word in order to form a different word.

superlative an adjective or adverb with '-est' on the end or 'most' in front of it; eg *thinnest, quickest, most beautiful.*

syllable a part of a word that contains a single vowel sound and that is pronounced as a unit.

tense the form of a verb which shows whether you are referring to the past, present, or future.

'that-' clause a clause starting with 'that', used mainly when reporting what someone has said; eg *She said **that she'd wash up for me***.

'to-' infinitive the base form of a verb preceded by 'to'; eg *to go, to have, to jump*.

transitive verb a verb which takes an object; eg *She's **wasting** her money*.

uncountable noun a noun which has only one form, takes a singular verb, and is not used with 'a' or numbers; eg *coal, courage, anger, help, fun*.

vowel a sound such as the ones represented in writing by the letters 'a', 'e', 'i', 'o' and 'u' which you pronounce with your mouth open, allowing the air to flow through it.

'wh-' word one of a group of words starting with 'wh-', such as 'what', 'when' or 'who', which are used in 'wh-' questions. 'How' is also called a 'wh-' word because it behaves like the other 'wh-' words.

Index